# GOD-INCIDENCES

## IN BOONE COUNTY

Bible references are quoted from the New International Version, 2011.

Published by
AKA-Publishing
Columbia, Missouri

AKA-Publishing

ISBN: 978-1-951960-00-1

# GOD-INCIDENCES
## IN BOONE COUNTY

*Stories of Extraordinary Encounters with God*

# JOHN GILLMAN
with Community Contributors

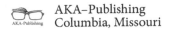 AKA–Publishing
Columbia, Missouri

# Table of Contents

# Foreword

*"Even when I am old and gray, do not forsake me, my God, till I declare your power to the next generation, your mighty acts to all who are to come." — Psalms 70:18*

What is a God-Incidence?

The following pages contain stories of events that have happened to me and others who live in Boone County, Missouri. Though some may see these events as having no cause, just coincidences, we think God was at work and prefer to call them God-Incidences. These stories have strengthened my faith and I hope they will do the same for you.

To my wife and kids: Pass along the faith and keep a heart of thankfulness; God has been good to our family.

To Harrisburg Christian Church and the Harrisburg Community: God is here with us in Boone County. All these events happened to people who live in our area. Feel free to ask them about their God-Incidences.

# Chapter One

## Does God Ever Speak?

The first two stories in this book are my favorite to tell. They remind me that God is able to communicate very clearly when He chooses. In "Postage Paid," I heard a very specific inner voice and in "The Peabody Miracle," the voice was out loud. If you have ever wondered if God still speaks words to people, I hope these accounts will answer your question.

"Family Matters" illustrates a different way that God communicates. Not in specific words, but in a way that touches our emotions, a strong urge or knowing that we ought to do something. Some might describe it as a calling. This has been the most common way that God has spoken to me. I often describe this communication as being led by the Holy Spirit. I think "Family Matters" illustrates the importance of responding to these leadings by God.

# Postage Paid

For several years in the days before the Internet, Kathleen and I would send out an annual Christmas letter to friends and extended family. It was early December and I had written the letter updating the readers on our year in review, and most importantly, what God had been doing in our lives and our reason for celebrating Christmas. We hoped the letter would be an encouragement to other Christians but also a way of sharing our faith with those who were not followers of Jesus.

As we started looking at our mailing list and counting the cost of copies, envelopes, and stamps, we realized that we didn't have the funds set aside to send out as many letters as we would like. We were about twenty to thirty dollars short, so we started having a conversation about who we could leave off the mailing. We had only been married a few years and there were people on the mailing list I barely knew from Kathleen's past and people on the list she barely knew from my past. I was suggesting we cut some people from her list, and she was suggesting a similar plan for my list and pretty soon the conversation of who to cut began to get a little more personal and tense. It was late anyway and we decided to sleep on it and talk about it the next day.

Of the two of us, I am usually the early riser. The next morning I got up before Kathleen and was getting ready for the day. As I was walking through the kitchen to have a time of prayer and Bible reading with the Lord, I passed the table where the mailing list was placed. I did not hear a voice out loud that I could have recorded, but in my mind/spirit,

I heard these words: *Don't cut anyone, I'll cover the cost.* I paused, and thought about what had just come into my mind. I assumed that the Holy Spirit was communicating with me, so I thanked God and when Kathleen woke up I said to her, "Don't cut anyone, I think God's going to cover the cost."

The next day in the mail we received an unexpected, anonymous money order for $750. Wow! One of our siblings commented that we could now send out videos instead of letters. This event certainly was affirmation of my belief that I *had* heard from God the day before. I have heard that 'voice' many times since that day, and though I would not propose that every thought or idea that pops into my head is from God, I do think it is reasonable to believe that this is one of the common ways that the Holy Spirit communicates to Christians.

This story also illustrates what I intend to mean with the term God–Incidence. The timing of the need, the 'voice,' and the check fit together so well that I am convinced they were orchestrated by God and not just a chance event. Not a coincidence with no apparent cause, but a God–Incidence.

# The Peabody Miracle

*Written by Anna Lewis*

Sonja Crozier desperately fought the levers of her zero-turn lawn mower as it slid sideways across the damp ground. The tires pushed across the steep, hilly driveway into the wet grass. She pushed and pulled frantically at the levers, but the mower continued to drift. Suddenly the back tire caught the edge of the driveway. The roll bar on the mower had been retracted earlier to avoid scraping against low branches. The machine flipped violently, leaving Sonja pinned underneath.

The seat pressed into her upper torso—950 pounds of force crushing her against the rocky ground, preventing her hand from reaching her phone. Sonja remembered with a pang of fear that she was not visible from the road and her husband would not be home for another two hours.

Sonja whispered twice, "God, please don't let me die," and then she lost her breath and slipped into unconsciousness.

That Monday had begun normally enough. It was the first day of June, but unseasonably chilly. Sonja, her foot booted from a recent surgery, had kissed her husband goodbye as he left for work. As the afternoon rolled around, Sonja thought she'd mow the lawn, though she'd been instructed to elevate her foot. A zero-turn mower wouldn't hurt her foot, she thought.

At a quarter to three, she decided to take a break from mowing. She turned back toward the house and started up the 600-foot driveway. Spotting a patch of weeds, she steered

5

toward the edge of the driveway. It was then that the mower turned over, trapping Sonja and leaving her without hope of rescue.

But God had other plans for Sonja.

Lewis Cox drove along Business 54 in a white sedan, headed back from work at HarbisonWalker International. An avid gardener, Lewis planned to stop by his shared garden outside of town before going home. As he reached the turn, he came to a stop. The turn would take him to the garden, it was where he always turned, but he couldn't turn. He simply sat at the intersection.

"It was like the left side of my brain was fighting with the right side, and I couldn't turn that day," he said. "I finally gave up and I told myself, 'well, I guess it looks like I am going home.'"

Continuing on, Lewis followed I-70 and Highway 63. Though Peabody Road is not his normal route to get home, on this day he turned west onto the gravel road. Lewis glanced up the steep first driveway. The overturned lawnmower up the Crozier's gravel lane gripped his vision. For a moment, Lewis felt like he was standing right over the mower, but he drove on.

As Lewis drove by, Sonja's body lay still, pinned under the mower. Her spirit, however, was elsewhere.

"I just remember being in a place that was really, really bright. It was so bright that all the people I saw—looking into this light—were silhouettes."

It was unlike any place she'd seen before.

"I thought, *boy, this place is full of children because they are skipping and running and jumping...* and the harder I looked, I was like, *no, these are adults. Some of these are adults and they are skipping."*

6

Sonja remembers being surrounded by a feeling of unconditional love and acceptance. Looking round upon the vastness of the place, she said she felt the weight of eternity.

"This world on Earth, even though it is our reality that we see, feel, and hear—it is like a mist. It is so fleeting, and it is so *not* what we should live for. That gigantic place where heaven is and where God is, is the actual place we need to live for," she said.

Lewis drove past one driveway, then another. Suddenly he was forced to stop.

"Turn and go back," said a voice. It was a clear male voice speaking to him.

Lewis obeyed, turning back to the Croziers' driveway and pulling in. He stopped short of the mower and walked up toward it, closing half the distance. Seeing nothing, he went back to the car, sticking his keys in the ignition.

As he was about to leave, he then heard a woman's voice right next to him, full of sorrow, say, "Come back! Come back!"

He got out of the car and walked all the way to the mower. Then he saw Sonja.

"She was solid black and purple as you can get," he said, "She was gone."

He grabbed the mower, trying to lift it with one hand so he could pull Sonja out. The mower was too heavy, but Lewis kept pushing.

"I just said a prayer to the Lord," recounted Lewis. "I said, 'Lord, you brought me all this way. You turned me back twice. Don't let it end like this.'"

• • •

Lewis looked down on Sonja's lifeless body. Suddenly, Lewis saw the "Breath of God" enter Sonja. Sonja gasped a breath and Lewis watched a dramatic color change take place over Sonja's skin.

Sonja looked up, seeing Lewis' straining arm, muscles and tendons popping as he held the mower. She tried to wiggle out.

Lewis was assured that this couldn't be a coincidental encounter. "God's got something special for you," he said. He finally managed to balance the mower on its side. "Don't move!" he said to Sonja and she stopped wiggling.

Lewis, certain that God had gotten them this far, believed that He would keep the mower from falling back down, ran to the car for his phone. Returning to the mower, Lewis held his phone up to his ear, talking to the 911 operator as he looked down at Sonja.

Sonja babbled incoherently at Lewis, her brain starved of oxygen, though Sonja thought she was speaking quite clearly.

Lewis unhooked the seatbelt and pushed the mower over as Sonja rolled out of the way. Sonja had a dislocated sternum and the bottom of both lungs were collapsed, but help was on the way. As the two strangers waited, Lewis continued to tell Sonja how he saw God breathe life into her.

Soon the ambulance arrived. Lewis crouched next to his white car, astonished and amazed at what God had done. As the paramedics looked her over, Sonja's voice returned, as did her husband.

As Joe pulled into the driveway, the paramedic turned to Sonja. "Does he usually get off at this time?"

Sonja realized that she had been under the mower for longer than she originally thought.

She was trapped under the mower without oxygen for two hours, yet retained her brainpower, her motor skills, her speech capabilities, and a memory of her trip to heaven.

Sonja needed very little medical treatment. She left the hospital and received in-home care from her sister, who was a registered nurse. Within the week, Sonja was healing well and her sister went home.

Joe and Sonja wanted to find her rescuer, but would have to go through a complicated process to make contact with him. Saturday morning after the accident they planned to call the police department and see if it would be possible to reach the man after Joe ran a few errands.

Soon after Joe left, she heard the doorbell ring.

"He forgot his keys," she thought. Slowly, she set aside her pillow and got to her feet. Painfully, she shuffled to the door. She peeked through the window, spotting a man about to leave in a familiar white car.

Tears streaming down her face, Sonja shouted, "I'm here! I'm home! Don't leave, don't leave!"

Lewis turned, relieved to see Sonja alive and well, and came inside at her invitation.

They sat and swapped stories—the stranger who heeded a voice, and the woman who went to heaven and back.

• • •

Sonja Crozier was saved that day. Crushed by 950 pounds for nearly two hours, she should have died. Sonja was saved by a God who put the right person in the right place at the right time, a God who told Lewis "go back," a God who breathed life into her breathless body. But Sonja wasn't the only one who was saved that day.

The day that Lewis Cox drove by that long gravel driveway, his faith was waning. Over the last year he had walked through the long and difficult process of watching his mother die from a prolonged illness. He was dealing with grief, but also some intense anger, having also discovered that someone close to him had been abused. The pressure that these and other situations were placing on Lewis's shoulders was becoming overwhelming. Those emotions paired with constant doses of evil coming from every news report had left Lewis wondering, *Where is God, does he even care?* But when he saw God at work in what he now calls the "Peabody Miracle," named after the road where it occurred, his life was changed.

"I know it was a miracle, and I know the divine Lord was a part of it, and he sent me there to help Sonja," said Lewis.

"I sit and think about it, and every time I get goosebumps," he said. "I have told so many people about this story because I feel like they need to hear it. The Lord is alive, he is well, and he wants to work in your life, my life, everybody's life. He does."

Sonja used to wonder why she'd been saved so miraculously.

"A really close friend of mine said, 'Why do you think God saved you that day?' So for about a year I felt really guilty. I felt really bad, because it was like, 'I am so unworthy of being saved,'" she said.

Sonja soon realized that the Peabody Miracle might not have been about her after all.

"After talking to Lewis and Lisa [Lewis' wife] on and off for a year, it finally dawned on me that God did not save me," Sonja said. "He saved them. He just used me to save them."

The Peabody Miracle began a lasting friendship between Lewis, Sonja, and their spouses. They recently celebrated together at one of the Cox children's weddings. They continue to give God glory for what happened. Sonja is comforted by the fact that the hardship she went through played a role in the Cox family and the direction of Lewis's faith. Lewis is humbled to think that God would use him to save Sonja's life and reminds Sonja that God has more in store for her. They continue to tell their story to others. Sonja works around cancer patients and has often used her story as evidence that God still does miracles.

# Family Matters

Collin McBride grew up on a farm south of Harrisburg. After High School graduation he went on to get a degree at Devry Institute and found employment first in Minneapolis and then in Kansas City. In the early nineties he was planning to return to Minneapolis to make a weekend visit to some friends from his previous employment. Collin's mother, Karen McBride, knew about his plans to travel for the weekend. What she didn't know was that Collin would wake up early and head up I-35 at four in the morning. She also didn't know that his life was going to be in danger.

Collin woke up well before his alarm and decided that he might as well get started; he had over six hours of travel in front of him. The dark spring morning was crisp and clear. The morning traffic was scarce and the roads were dry, so it was a complete surprise to Collin when he hit a patch of black ice while crossing a bridge in northern Missouri.

His car skidded out of control and slammed against one of the concrete sides of the bridge, deploying both airbags and bending the hood straight up in front of the windshield. The impact knocked Collin's glasses to the back seat and spun the car into the middle of the road facing northbound traffic. Disoriented and with vision impaired, Collin could still see the lights of an eighteen-wheeler coming toward the bridge. The front fender was bent in such a way that the car could not be steered.

Back in Harrisburg, God was communicating with Karen. She woke up before her alarm with a jolt and sat straight up in bed. Impressed on her spirit was an urgent sense that she needed to pray for Collin's safety even though it was still dark out. Wide awake, she began to pray.

On I-35 as the eighteen-wheeler approached, Collin was given a calmness and clarity of mind. He was able to re-start the car. It wouldn't turn, but because of the angle the car was sitting, he was able to drive it forward to the shoulder and out of the way of the approaching semi. Collin then got out and bent the fender back enough to allow him to steer and maneuver the car up the road to the nearest truck stop. He found a pay phone and called home. His praying mother picked up the phone.

After hearing about what had happened to Collin, Karen realized that her feeling of urgency at such an early hour in the morning was no coincidence. Her prayers were needed and answered.

A couple of years later, Collin received a similar communication from God. Collin's father, Craig McBride was nearing the end of a long battle with brain cancer. Collin was still working in Kansas City and trying to visit home as often as possible. The brain tumor progressed, and the family grieved as Craig's body began to lose different functions. Six months prior he had been unable to get out of bed. Among other things, during the progression, he had stopped speaking and one of his eyes was no longer able to open.

On August tenth of 1994, as Collin sat at work, he felt an urgent calling placed on his spirit. He knew he needed to go home right away and that his dad's time was imminent. He simply said to his boss, "I've got to go home." He went to his apartment and got clothes for the funeral, and jumped into his car and headed back home to Route J.

Collin walked into the house a little after five that evening. Karen was surprised but thankful to have him there. Craig had been unresponsive all day. Around eleven that night with Collin and Karen in the room, Craig had a moment of resurgence. He opened both eyes, and though he couldn't speak, was alert, nodded at them, and communicated through his eyes. They sensed that the message being communicated was, "I'm okay to go on to Heaven, I know you aren't alone." It was a deep and touching moment for both of them. After Craig's moment of clarity, he drifted back to sleep and joined the Lord that morning at three.

Collin is still moved by the memory of that night and thanks God for the 'calling' to go home.

He states, "That is the closest thing to a miracle that I have ever witnessed."

# Chapter Two

## Will God Provide?

The following stories all involve the provision of God. Though I would point to God as the ultimate provider in all situations, these stories seem to speak a direct message that God is aware of our specific circumstances and will provide what we need. As with many God–Incidences we are left saying, "What are the odds of that happening?" These stories cause me to stand back and chuckle at the hand of God.

If you are dealing with financial hardship, I hope that through these stories you will hear God whisper, "It's going to be okay, I see what you are going through."

# The Love Offering

Back in the nineties when Kathleen and I were living in Centralia, I spent several weeks in the summer and early fall preaching as pulpit supply for Harrisburg Christian Church. I had been filling the pulpit off and on for several years and had developed a good rapport with the congregation. Following my stint of substitution in Harrisburg, God brought Harrisburg Christian Church a pastor, and I went back to Centralia where I taught biology in the public school system Monday through Friday, and Sunday School at my church each week.

I had little contact with Harrisburg Christian Church for the next few months other than their monthly newsletter, *The Beacon*. I noticed in the January edition an announcement saying there would be a love offering taken up for the Gillman family. Kathleen and I were not experiencing any financial hardship at the time, so I was surprised! Though we didn't understand the purpose of the love offering we were grateful, especially when we received a check in the mail for $500! To a young family on a tight budget (school teacher and homemaker), with two children at that time, this was an unexpected treat. Kathleen and I sat on the couch excited to discuss the ways we could spend the money.

A couple of days after receiving the check, I left for a science convention and while I was there I got a phone call from Kathleen. She told me we had received our heating bill in the mail. At the time we were on a 'budget billing plan' set up so that we would pay the same amount each month based on estimated yearly costs. Once a year the gas company would even up and bill us the remaining balance or give us a credit. This was our month to even up. I asked Kathleen, "How much is it?"

Gas prices had gone up that year and it had been a cold winter in our hundred-year-old house. Turned out, we owed a little over $500. Now we understood why we needed that love offering. God knew what was coming and He took care of us through Harrisburg Christian Church.

To the eyes of the faithless, this story might just be labeled a coincidence. To the eyes of a pessimist, they might say, "That's just my luck, I get this money and now I've got to give it to the gas company." But to our eyes, this was yet another time where God has shown that He is real, that He cares and provides for us, and that three months prior to us getting a bill he knew what we would need and prompted His people in another town to serve Him and us. We call this a God–Incidence.

# A Timely Offer

When you first meet Theresa Bradford, you'd never know that she has traveled such a difficult road to get to the Harrisburg area. She has a bubbly personality and a loud, infectious laugh. She loves to praise God and can be found most Sundays helping lead the worship at Harrisburg Christian Church.

Theresa moved to the Harrisburg area to escape an unhealthy marriage relationship and to get a fresh start. As a homemaker, she was fully dependent on her husband's income. The move was difficult for multiple reasons, finances being one of them. At the time of the move in 2009, she still had two of her five children living with her. She was homeschooling the boys and began trying to make ends meet by putting together gun parts for a local gun manufacturer and by cleaning a home.

Theresa has been and is still being plagued by multiple health issues. In 2011 her back was the latest culprit. The up and down motion necessary for her weekly house-cleaning job was putting a strain on her lower back and leaving her in debilitating pain the next day. Finally her doctor informed her that she was going to have to stop the cleaning service. Her body could not handle the movement. Later that day in tears she cried out to God, "What am I going to do, Lord? I needed that four hundred dollars a month to make ends meet."

Theresa thought back to the financial security she had when she was living with her husband, but when she thought of the abuse and infidelity, she was reminded that the boundary she set was necessary. The decision to separate from her husband was a step of faith. She entrusted her need to the Lord.

That week, Theresa received a call from the city of Armstrong. Over the last year or so, she had been attending city council meetings, and had recently lost a run for council by only four votes. The council, knowing her desire to help the Armstrong community be a better place, thought of her when an opening came up. "Theresa, we need someone to fill the role of City Collector, and we'd like you to consider taking the job. We could really use you…. Oh, by the way, it pays four hundred dollars a month." Theresa took the job and also the 'hint from God' that He heard her prayer and was providing for her.

# Giving in Faith

When I first met Scott Ashton, he was a college baseball coach at Hannibal LeGrange College; he had come to interview for an area representative position with Fellowship of Chrisitan Athletes (FCA). The position was a "raise your own salary through donations" job and the following story is one that built Scott's confidence in a God who provides.

In 1997, Scott had come under two convictions that he believed to be from God: One, to be debt-free going into marriage, and two, to begin to tithe off his income. Tithing is a Christian practice that started thousands of years ago in which a person would take the first and best of their income or herd/produce, and offer it to God. The word tithe means a tenth and many Christians today give a tenth of their income back to God as a way of honoring Him and expressing trust in His future provision. In order to be debt free, Scott would need to pay off his vehicle debt. He owed $2300 on a white GMC Sonoma truck. That may not seem like too overwhelming of a debt, but his salary as a coach at a private college was pretty meager. It was going to take a while to pay down the debt, especially if he started tithing. Scott had also fallen in love with a local girl named Susan Lee and they had recently become engaged.

Would God provide a way for Scott to pay off the vehicle even as he reduced his available funds by ten percent? Scott was attending Cornerstone Baptist Church in Hannibal and learning that tithing was a very tangible way to actively demonstrate your faith. Scott wanted to be a man of faith as he looked forward to a life together with Susan, and hopefully children.

The decision to give a tenth of his income to the local church also carried some additional baggage for Scott. Though he remembers his mom writing checks to the church, he had grown up in a home where his dad was very outspoken about religious people always being out for your money. When a TV preacher would be on, his dad, using very colorful language would talk about how the preacher was stealing old ladies' money. Memories of his dad's comments were going through Scott's mind as he began to write tithing checks. Scott prayed, "God I'm going to put you first in my finances and trust you to help me get debt-free before marriage."

A few weeks later, Scott got a call from his mother. "Scott, I was going through some old papers and was just reminded that you have an old whole life policy from your grandfather. You can either cash it out or keep investing in it, what would you like to do?

"Cash it out." Scott said. He received the check and to Scott's surprise, the amount was for $2350. Scott looked at his $2300 truck bill and knew God was affirming his trust in Him. Scott likes to remind people that God gave him a clear title and a tank of gas.

Keep an eye out for Scott, the life insurance story was a faith builder for him. He went on to accept the position of area representative for FCA where God has used him to encourage thousands of coaches and athletes. He has seen God provide his salary through the donations of others for the last eighteen years. Scott and Susan are happily married and still excited to make the first check they write each month a tithing check.

# APA Style

*Written by Cindy Roller*

I have two associate's degrees, and although I had never completed a bachelor's degree it had always been on my "bucket list." After I retired from the military and my last child was a senior in college, it seemed as though it was the right season to work toward this goal. I looked into a few different schools and investigated who would allow the most transfer credits, and settled into an online program.

I took three credit hours the first session to get my feet wet. It went well, and because patience is not a virtue I possess, I enrolled for eighteen credit hours for the next ten-week session. Working forty-plus hours a week while taking eighteen hours of senior level courses was challenging, to say the least.

During one particularly stressful week I had three significant papers due. I texted Vickie Spry to let her know I wasn't going to make it to Bible study that evening. I have always been very independent, struggle with constantly wanting to be in control, and rarely ask for help. But I felt encouraged to text Vickie again and ask her to add me to our group's prayer list, and admitted that I was feeling a bit overwhelmed.

The online program required a lot of writing and required following the APA Manual of Style for formatting. I enjoy writing, but just could not get the hang of APA formatting. I didn't understand it. All of the resources I could find were online, and honestly were just not sinking in. I felt that if I could just find a "how-to" book, a real book with pages and everything, that maybe it would help my comprehension. I asked God to help me settle down and concentrate. I sat at the kitchen table with my computer, feeling very frustrated.

My frustration led to avoidance and procrastination. I noticed a cup in the living room that needed to be put into the sink. Right now. Then I noticed a blanket that needed to go into the guest bedroom. Again, this needed to happen at this very moment. While in the bedroom, I saw the binder that has my Christmas card list (still on the bed from Christmas time—this was now April). Of course right now would be an appropriate time to put it away on the bookshelf downstairs, because otherwise I may have to work on at least one of my dreaded papers!

I took the binder downstairs and tried to put in into the same spot where it has been stored for many years. It wouldn't go. I pushed over a couple of books that seemed to be crowding it, but no luck. It still would not go into its spot. It seemed like it was running into something. I reached into the space where my binder needed to go, and felt a small spiral bound book. Hmm. I pulled it out. It was a book that I had never seen before—ever. And the title was *An Easy Guide to APA Style*. I caught my breath! Seriously? WHERE did this come from? I had to smile—I knew God placed it right where I needed it.

Why did I just happen to put away my Christmas card binder today? Why did I admit that I was feeling overwhelmed and ask for prayer? So that God could help me, and remind me that HE is in control!

Oh, by the way. I asked my son if he had ever seen this APA formatting book. He said, "Hey, I got that book when I was a freshman—I haven't seen that thing in years. Where did you find it?"

# The Van from God

I have always driven inexpensive vehicles. When I married Kathleen, I married into car payments and the new 1993 Saturn that we drove was the nicest vehicle I had ever owned. At that time in our young marriage I was driving an old Dodge Colt which later bit the dust, followed by an old Buick Century that also died. After the Buick we decided to be a one car family for a while because we really didn't have the funds for a second car. Fortunately I lived close enough to the school to ride my bike to work.

My insurance agent and friend Jed Angel was talking to a client that year about his car insurance and the client said, "I've got a car that I'd like to sell or give away or something like that." Jed clarified that the client had said, "Give away" and told him that he had a family in mind. I met this gentleman for the first time on a Saturday morning. He handed me the keys to a car. The Honda Accord was gassed up, cleaned up, freshly oiled, extra fluids included, and then took rank as the second nicest car I had ever owned. By the way, the man was Mike Harvey who served as the pastor of Harrisburg Christian Church from 2001-2003.

Both cars were running great, but when Kathleen became pregnant with child number three, we realized that our family of five—three in car seats—was not going to fit in either car. Though I am tentative to use the word *need*, we had reached a point where we needed a van. The problem was, we did not have room in our tight budget for van payments.

I kept track of our spending budget and felt like I did a pretty good job of knowing what money was coming in and what money was going out. I would review the monthly bank statements. As the months went by, I noticed there was a discrepancy between my records and the bank's records. The bank seemed to think that I had more money in my account than I thought I did. I tried to get the two amounts to balance, but was unsuccessful. I ignored the money for a while thinking that we must have purchased something that I hadn't been billed for yet, but each month kept showing a discrepancy. At one point I brought up the issue with the bank, I said "I think there is a mistake and I don't have as much money as you think I do." They said they were going to trust their records over mine which I appreciated, so I left the issue alone. There was unaccounted extra money in our checking account to the tune of three thousand dollars. I assume someone was making anonymous deposits.

Kathleen and I decided to trade in the Honda and use the extra money in our checking account to purchase a van. It was just the right amount! We saw this as provision from God and began to refer to the vehicle as our "Van from God."

Within the year, my brother-in-law David was blessed with a good stock deal and bought a new van. He gave us his old one which was five years and 50,000 miles younger than the Dodge we had just purchased. We considered the newer Ford our "Upgraded Van from God."

Was God providing or were people providing? I guess I would say it's both. God used people to provide for us. Over the years we have received multiple unsolicited gifts and thoughtful gestures, many of them met very specific needs that we had. Sometimes the gift came even before we knew we had the need. Over the years I have lost count of the amount of times God has provided by prompting someone to help us or offer something to us. We have been given food, a computer, clothing, toys, unexpected money, vacations, vacation spots, vacation money, a swingset, vehicles, beds, gift cards, and more.

It has been very humbling to be in need and to be on the receiving end of someone's generosity, but I've realized that there are two sides to the giving stories. There are times when I see a need and am prompted by God to be generous towards others and when they receive my gift well, I feel blessed and used by God. Kathleen and I have tried to be good receivers and humbly accept what others offer as often as we can.

# God's Shovel

Someone once told me that "God's shovel is bigger than our shovel." As we seek to be generous and give to others, God shovels back generously to us. I found that principle illustrated in the following event that happened while we were living in Centralia.

God impressed on me a need in our community. A family was struggling financially and I felt that our praise team at First Baptist Church should take some groceries to them. We agreed to all put in some money, go together to the store, purchase groceries, and deliver them. I kept some spending money in a jar on hand that was saved for special occasions. I pulled out forty dollars from the jar to take to the store. As I was stepping away from the jar I hesitated. I asked myself, is that too much? It was half the money in the jar and I didn't know when I'd be making another deposit to the cash drawer. No, I thought, God will cover us. He's got lots of money and will provide what we need; He always has. So I took the forty dollars.

By the end of the shopping trip, others had joined me in donating money, we purchased eighty dollars in groceries for the family. One of the men in the group pulled me aside and gave me ten dollars back. He said "Here, you didn't need to give that much."

At church that Sunday I was given a surprise gift of a hundred dollars from the church for pastor appreciation month for my fill-in role as worship leader a few months back. I told the congregation that day, "God's shovel is bigger than ours. I gave forty dollars to God this week and He gave me back one hundred ten."

Growing up around followers of Jesus has placed me in the path of many generous people. I feel I have been the recipient much more than the participant of this generosity, but I have continually seen the shovel principle ring true. Those who continually seek to bless others seem to continually be blessed by God. I don't think that is just a coincidence.

# Help from the Snowstorm

In 2002, Kathleen's mother had broken her ankle. Kathleen wanted to go and help her, so she took our three young children and headed to Saint Joseph, Missouri for a few days. At the time I was teaching and coaching basketball in Centralia and since it was a weekday, I wasn't able to join the rest of the family for the trip.

While Kathleen was in Saint Joseph, our middle child Ann Elizabeth, who was three at the time began complaining about her legs hurting. Kathleen checked her legs and noticed that her joints were swollen, so she and her father, Gene Sanders, took Ann Elizabeth to the emergency room. By the time they got all checked in, the swelling had gone down and Ann Elizabeth was giggling and running around and having no problems. She was quickly released and sent home.

That night a blizzard hit the area. Everyone was advised to stay in, schools closed, travel was impossible for the vehicles at the Sanders' home. They were snowed in. The next day the swelling returned to Ann Elizabeth's legs, now with purplish spots. Kathleen needed to get her to the emergency room, but the roads were not cleared.

Fortunately, Kathleen's brother David, who also lives in Saint Joseph was available and had a four-wheel drive truck. When David came to pick up Kathleen and Ann Elizabeth, he took one look at her legs and said, "That's HSP, my son had that last year." As soon as they got to the emergency room, David began to explain to the doctors and technicians that Ann Elizabeth had HSP, a rare autoimmune disease.

If you've never heard of Henoch–Schonlein Purpura or HSP, join the club, because none of the medical personnel at the emergency room had heard of HSP either. Fortunately, David is a professional salesman and can be very convincing. The medical personnel began to run tests on Ann Elizabeth including tests for HSP. Sure enough, it was HSP and the hospital was able to make a quick diagnosis and begin treatment. She was admitted and immediately started on fluids and steroids to combat the disease.

When I look back at this event in our family's life, I see God's provision. I think of all the pieces that fell into place in order for Ann Elizabeth to get a quick diagnosis and effective treatment. Had it not snowed, David wouldn't have been there to help. Had Kathleen stayed in Boone County, we would have gone to a different hospital and who knows how much time and how many tests it would have taken to properly diagnose Ann Elizabeth. Many pieces of the puzzle had to fall together at just the right time in order to keep further complications at bay. We do not credit all these events to coincidence, we call it yet another God–Incidence in our lives and thank God for providing a healing path for our daughter.

# Chapter Three:

## Does God Answer Prayers?

Yes, God does answer prayers, as these stories will illustrate, but I must admit, why some prayers get answered with a 'Yes' and others with a 'No' or 'Wait' has been and continues to be mysterious to me. As I was growing up in a farming household, it seemed we were always praying that it would either start raining or stop raining. Sometimes, as I looked out the window at the pouring rain and new streams running down our driveway and flooding a freshly planted field, I wondered if praying even made a difference.

Over the years I have become convinced that prayer does make a difference, but I am also convinced that the purpose of prayer is not to get what we want out of God, but to develop a relationship with Him. Part of that relationship involves taking our needs to God in prayer as illustrated in the "Lord Please Show Me" story. It also involves working alongside the Lord with our prayers which is what I think Cecil-Mae Nichols experienced in the "No Crash?" story.

When I started serving as the pastor at Harrisburg Christian Church I received a clear message from the Lord. I heard (in my spirit) the Lord say, "Always keep prayer at the forefront of this ministry." I have tried not to forget that message over the last sixteen years. I hope these stories will be yet another reminder to keep praying.

# Lord Please Show Me

On several occasions, our family experienced God answering prayer while Kathleen was a stay-at-home mom and our three children were preschool age. We were living in the town of Centralia within walking distance of our local park.

One day our son John Michael had lost his favorite sunglasses while playing in the park. Kathleen went back with the children and looked all over the play area and did not find his sunglasses. On the walk back home, very discouraged, Kathleen prayed, "God you know where the sunglasses are, will you remind me or show me where they are?" As she prayed she immediately had a picture come to her mind of John Michael playing with some sticks the day before. By this time they were close to the house, so she put the children in the van and drove back to the area that had come to mind. Sure enough, there were the sunglasses, lying right next to the sticks.

In a similar instance, our daughter Maddie couldn't find her favorite set of toy horses. Kathleen and the children looked all over the house but could not find them. Finally Kathleen sat down with the children and said, "Let's pray, 'God you know where the horses are and you can see them, please remind someone, put it in our minds where they are.'" At the very moment that Kathleen said, "In Jesus name, Amen." John Michael stood up and went behind the couch and retrieved the horses. God had reminded him exactly where he had put them at an earlier time.

Notice that we lose a lot of things in our family. My mother-in-law had been visiting us and when she left, she forgot her purse. She lived three hours from us so as soon as Kathleen realized it, she tried to call her mom's cell phone but couldn't get through. Kathleen sat down with the kids to pray. She wanted a specific prayer and noticed the sunglasses in her mother's purse. "God," she prayed, "please let her need her sunglasses and realize she left her purse."

It was an overcast day, but as Kathleen was praying she got a phone call. It was her mother asking; "Did I leave my purse?" When she got back to our house, Kathleen asked what caused her to think of it. She replied, "You wouldn't know it by looking at the sky now, but when I was out on the road, I needed my sunglasses!" We were thankful to God for letting the light shine and answering Kathleen's prayer.

• • •

One night our son was upset by a nightmare and was crying. Reaching his room first, I tried to console him, but to no avail. Kathleen entered the room and began to pray over him, "God, you are the God of all peace. I pray that your peace will fill John Michael, that you will calm his Spirit in the name of Jesus." Our son was immediately calm and at peace. It was amazing to be in the room and witness the transformation in our young son.

The reason Kathleen was praying out loud with the kids was because of her desire for our children to see that God answers our prayers.

I am thankful for a praying wife and thankful that my children and I have had the opportunity to see her example of taking needs to God, asking specifically, and having full faith that God can provide. We have seen God answer many prayers over the years. The unique factors about these stories illustrate that the answers were immediate and specific to my wife's requests. I think they were more than coincidences.

# Pool Table Prayer

I have always liked to play pool (billiards) and I was so excited when some friends of ours in Centralia offered to give us their pool table if we would take it apart and get it out of their basement. It was a three-slate table in good condition, but not an easy task to move. Not having a truck, I borrowed my friend Lynn Miller's truck and Lynn. We backed the truck into the garage of the home and began to disassemble the pool table and load it up. which took quite a while.

Once we got the table loaded, we saw that it had started to sprinkle outside. Fortunately, I had remembered to bring a tarp which was in the cab of the truck. As I went to get it and explained my intentions to Lynn, he said "You can put the tarp on or just trust God to stop the rain."

"I think I have a little more faith in this tarp than God stopping the rain," I replied. Lynn is a great storyteller, handiman, minister, former auctioneer, and salesman. But my favorite "Lynn quality" is his faith. He has experienced God–Incidences on multiple occasions and loves to tell about it.

He started in on his sermon. "Well, stopping the rain is nothing for God, I've seen him do way more amazing things than that! He changes lives, there's nothing more amazing than that, he changed me, I've seen him change dozens of people, the rain is nothing...." He kept going while I was fiddling with the tarp.

If there is such a thing as a "Christian dare," I was feeling it as Lynn spoke. He didn't state these words, but I was feeling like he was saying: "What's the matter with you John, don't you have any faith in God?" I looked at Lynn, stopped messing with the tarp and said a brief, out loud prayer: "Okay, God, we really like this pool table: please don't let it get damaged." Lynn stopped his sermon, I folded the tarp up and placed it back in the truck and we started heading down the gravel road toward the blacktop. We were about five miles from my home.

As we drove down the gravel road to the highway, the sprinkles became fewer and fewer and by the time we had traveled about a mile, the sprinkles had stopped. We drove the few miles to my home and backed up to the front porch. We unloaded the table piece by piece into the newly named "pool room" in our old home.

The attention-getting part of this story for both Lynn and me happened as we grabbed the last piece of the pool table from the truck bed. As soon as we started to step on the covered wrap-around porch, it began to rain, not a light sprinkle like before, but a downpour. It was as if God had held back the rain for just the moment when the pool table would be in the clear. Lynn and I stood on the porch as the rain poured down and just looked at each other in awe. "I can't believe that just happened." I said. But, I want you as the reader to know that I do believe God changed the weather that day on our behalf. I believe he answered our prayer.

# "I Need Help"

When it comes to physical challenges, there isn't much Al Quevreaux hasn't tried and succeeded at. He has been a Marine, a boxer, a hunter, and a hiker. But since his Parkinson's diagnosis ten years ago, he has watched his physical abilities slowly fade away. It has become a challenge to even get up from a chair and move across the room. He has lost a lot of control and strength in his muscles.

A few years ago Al was outside between his garage and shed. As he got about halfway across the driveway, the support brace on his right leg came loose, causing him to lose his balance, falling to the concrete. Al wasn't going to be able to stand without pulling up on something. He looked ahead into the barn and spotted his ATV parked and ready. Al uses his ATV to idle through the woods by his home and go back to one of his favorite places overlooking Silver Fork Creek. He knew if he could get to the ATV, he could use the crate on the back end to pull himself up.

From a sitting position while using both of his shaking arms he began to push up his torso and scoot his rear about six inches at a time toward the ATV. It was about thirty feet away. Finally, after about twenty minutes, when he got to the crate, he reached up with both hands and tried to pull himself up. After a couple of failed attempts, the Marine came out in him. With a look of determination and grit he grabbed the crate and pulled with all his might. It just wasn't enough and he fell back to the concrete, exhausted. Al remembers his exact prayer: "Lord, I need help, I can't make it without you." Grabbing the crate once again, Al pulled himself right up. Exhausted and now thankful, Al knew that God had answered his prayer.

As I have gotten to know Al, one of my favorite lines is how he describes his coming to Jesus. He says "Jesus gave me the best knock-out punch I ever received, hoo–hoo!" Al's answered prayer for help was yet another time that Al was thankful for the Lord's presence in his life.

# The Musk Ox Prayer

A few years ago, Josh Byrd went on an adventure of a lifetime, a musk ox hunt in northern Canada. What started out as a four-day hunt turned into a trying and difficult journey and a unique God–Incidence.

The conditions were brutal. The temperatures ranged from a high of zero to a low of negative seventy. Travel was on sleds being pulled roughly by snowmobiles. Housing was in various uninsulated ten by ten foot plywood huts.

Josh's companions were two indigenous guides and a fellow hunter (we will call him Harry) that he met when he got to Canada. Josh and Harry had a lot in common, but Josh realized soon into the trip that Harry was not a fellow believer. He was outspoken about being an unbeliever and Josh left the spiritual topic alone in their conversations.

Musk ox hunting involves riding the snowmobile-pulled-sleds along the open frozen range looking for tracks and the black dots of distant oxen along the landscape. It is essential to have good visibility and no falling snow. The weather was not favorable, and after day four, there were no sightings and two disappointed hunters. The men had the option of staying until they filled their hunting tags and they decided to extend the trip. They refueled and resupplied and returned to the wild. They were traveling up to fifty miles a day, but still no sightings. When they finally saw some tracks, the weather slowed their pace and falling snow covered them up.

Day nine came. Frustration was high, one of the snowmobiles had broken, and a storm limited visibility to under a hundred yards. The men had been confined to the cabin for several days because of the weather. Finally, Josh spoke up, somewhat out of frustration and partly out of faith. "Okay, Harry, we've been doing this your way. Today we are doing it my way."

Harry scoffed, "Whatever."

Although Josh had prayed silently many times during the trip, this time he prayed out loud. "Lord, please help us, we're tired and frustrated and we'd like to shoot an ox."

Within minutes, the men began to see a break in the storm and they watched as the storm cleared out. They stepped out of the cabin but still had the problem of the snowmobile that wouldn't start. "Oh great!" said Harry sarcastically.

Josh prayed out loud again. "Lord, please help this snowmobile to start." A few pulls later and the snowmobile was running fine. The men got on the sleds. Within ninety minutes they had located not one, but two bull musk ox. Josh shot one with a bow and Harry shot one with a gun.

Soon afterward Harry ran up to Josh and said something like; "Hey, I'm not saying I'm becoming a Christian or anything, but what happened back there was real. Something different happened when you prayed."

Josh saw God get both hunters' attention that day. As Josh shared his story with me, I was reminded that the God we serve has control over every part of this planet and he can move storms, start snowmobiles, herd musk ox, get the attention of those who do not believe, and encourage those of us who do—by answering prayer. We serve a great God!

# No Crash?

"Pray for Kurt and Debbie now!" Cecil-Mae Nichols was driving past Rangeline Road as she traveled from her Millersburg home into Columbia on Route WW. She was alone in the car, but a male voice was speaking to her. She heard the voice over her right shoulder. It was loud and demanding and clearly telling her to pray for her son and his bride.

Kurt and Debbie also traveled into Columbia for work, and would cut north on Rangeline road so Kurt could start early at his job with the city, and Debbie could take the car to her tech support job at the Orthopedic Foundation for Animals.

Cecil-Mae had offered up many prayers for her sons. She and her husband Darryl had been blessed with four children, all boys, and all full of energy. If you aren't familiar with the rural, redneck culture of Harrisburg, Missouri, picture a yard and shop filled with a group of ornery teenage males wearing greasy jeans, boots, and T-shirts; country music playing while the latest hunting story is being told; and the latest broken vehicle is being fixed. Cecil-Mae had prayed many a prayer for her boys safety and decisions, but never before had she heard this voice.

Cecil prayed for Kurt and Debbie and since she traveled the road frequently, she began to use the Rangeline crossroad as a daily reminder to pray for her third son. It wasn't until a few weeks later that she would discover why she was commanded to pray.

At a family gathering later that month, Debbie asked Kurt if he had told his mother about their recent incidents. Kurt proceeded to share the following stories.

It had been quite a month of country road driving for Kurt. On two different occasions earlier in the month, Kurt hit a deer. In both instances, the antlers of the bucks not only damaged the body of the truck, but punctured the radiator. As soon as Kurt got the truck fixed from the first deer, he was making a claim on the second. The event was so unique that State Farm sent an adjuster out to make sure it wasn't a duplicate claim. Following the second repair, Kurt and Debbie experienced two unexplainable events together in the truck.

The first took place in the evening. Kurt and Debbie were on their way to Columbia to have dinner. Traveling across Highway WW within a mile of Rangeline Road, they crested a hill a little after five o'clock to discover a herd of deer in the road. There were animals in both lanes. There was no time to stop and no place to turn where they could avoid hitting a deer. Debbie closed her eyes and Kurt started to hit the brakes and braced for impact. He was about to hit his third deer that month.

Then amazingly, no impact happened. As the truck came to a stop, Debbie opened her eyes and looked back to see the deer, still in the middle of the road. They paused the truck for a few minutes to catch their breath. Kurt simply stated, "I can't explain what just happened." But he was thankful, and believed that they had just received help from above. The Nichols had listed their truck in the Auto Trader Magazine and had a buyer coming to pick up the vehicle that weekend. It made it through a herd of deer without a scratch. But that wasn't the last miraculous event that the two would experience.

The buyer couldn't make it that weekend due to a family emergency, so he rescheduled for a couple of weeks later. Kurt and Debbie parked the vehicle, not wanting to risk any more accidents. But a week later on Monday morning, the truck was needed, it was raining buckets and the truck was more dependable on the slick roads. The two turned down Rangeline Road towards their Columbia jobs. Up ahead they could see a car coming down a driveway to their right. The visibility at the end of the driveway was blocked by a tree. Debbie was just cautioning Kurt, "be careful, she can't see us," when the car pulled out onto the road right in front of them. When the driver of the car realized she hadn't seen a truck coming, she hit her brakes, but by that time her car was far enough into both lanes that there wasn't room on either side of the narrow road for the truck. Debbie again closed her eyes. Kurt slammed on the brakes and braced for impact.

Again, there was no crash. Somehow, the truck slid around the car. There was no contact with the vehicle and the truck did not hit the steep ditch. As Kurt and Debbie paused in the road on the other side of the car, the driver gave a brief wave to them and drove away. The Nichols again gave thanks to God and were happy to see that the next day, the tree at the end of the driveway was cut down.

Kurt is no stranger to driving. His dad was a trucker, and he grew up driving vehicles of all sorts. At the time of these incidents, he was driving heavy equipment for the City of Columbia, and at the time of this writing, he was working as an over-the-road trucker. Kurt could not explain why no accident occurred on either occasion. There must have been help from God.

As his mother, Cecil-Mae heard these stories for the first time, she realized that the voice she heard telling her to pray for Kurt and Debbie around Rangeline Road matches up with the timing of these incidents. She understood why her prayer was needed and thanks God for using her prayers to help keep her family safe.

# Chapter Four

## Does God Give Specific Assignments?

One of my favorite verses in the Bible comes from Paul's letter to the Christians in Ephesus:

> *"For we are God's handiwork, created in Christ Jesus to do good works, which God prepared in advance for us to do." — Ephesians 2:10*

I believe the following stories illustrate some of those good works that God specifically called me and some other individuals in our community to accomplish.

Sometimes I hear others express frustration toward a community, they see a need and say, "Why isn't somebody doing something about that?" I have felt that same frustration at times, and agree that sometimes others do not meet a need that they ought to meet. However, I'm beginning to realize that sometimes I see a need that I think should be obvious to everyone, but it's not because it is a specific assignment to me from God. Perhaps it's not a coincidence that you see unmet needs that others don't; it might be an assignment from God to you.

I'd encourage you to offer yourself to the Lord and say a simple prayer like, "Lord, I want to be involved in the good works that you have prepared for me, what would you like for me to do today?"

# McDonalds Meeting

For several years while I was teaching at Centralia, I sponsored an FCA (Fellowship of Christian Athletes) group. One year I had a student leader that wanted to learn to share his faith with others so I offered to help him learn by doing. He and I would invite other students to meet us after school at McDonalds for an ice cream sundae and a conversation about the Christian faith and how to begin a relationship with God. We tried to do this once a week and each looked for students that might be interested whom we could invite to join us.

During lunch one week I was sitting across from a substitute teacher who was a former Centralia student. As we caught up and spoke, I sensed the Holy Spirit prompting me to invite this man to join us after school. It was our day of the week to meet and so far we didn't have a guest invited to our meeting. I often get these promptings from the Holy Spirit which are often followed by what I would label as "pre-witnessing jitters." I get afraid of how other people might react if I bring up the topic of faith. As I thought about inviting the substitute teacher to join us, I got the jitters. I thought to myself, "Nah, he wouldn't be interested."

But the prompting didn't go away. I still felt like the Holy Spirit wanted me to invite him.

Not wanting to completely disobey God, I threw out some conditions in a quick prayer. I said, "Okay, God, when the bell rings, I'm going to stop by the restroom. If he goes in there too, I'll invite him." Sure enough, he headed to the restroom and I invited him to join us as we were washing our hands. He agreed to meet us. The conversation at McDonalds went well. He was interested in the information we shared and seemed to understand the message.

What struck me about the whole incident was the comment he made as we were leaving the restaurant. He said, "You know, this is so weird that you brought this up today. I was just thinking about this last night."

It was another reminder to me to respond to the promptings of the Holy Spirit. Even if I think it may be unlikely that a person would be interested in talking about their spiritual life, I never know what they may have been thinking of the day before. I don't think our meeting that day was just a coincidence, I think it was an assignment from God.

# A Rainstorm Message

I think God used a specific rainstorm to get my attention and remind me of the importance of prayer.

During my first year as pastor of Harrisburg Christian Church I made an intentional effort to get to know the members of the church as quickly as I could. Carol Hughes put together a book for me that contained not only the directory picture of each family, but also family information she knew and space for notes that I could make as I got to know the families.

I also made a concerted effort to keep prayer at the forefront of the ministry and to pray for each of the families on a regular basis. One month I made a thirty-day commitment to start off each morning by flipping through my book and praying for each of the Harrisburg families before I started on anything else for the day.

One morning during that thirty day commitment I knelt down with my directory in front of me to begin praying. I looked out the living room window and decided it would be a good morning to go for a jog. As I thought about going for a jog before I prayed, I felt a twinge of guilt because I had told God that I would pray for the congregation as my first priority each morning. I wrestled with the decision for a bit and then decided to go ahead and jog. I justified the decision in my mind by saying, "I'll pray for the congregation while I jog and then I will come back to the house and check the directory to see if I missed anyone." I didn't quite feel right about the decision, but I put on my shoes and headed out the door.

I ran out the back door and started down the alley. After going about a half a block I began to feel rain drops. By the time I had gone another block, the rain had become steady. I looked up and thought, "I'd better go back." I turned around and started running back. The rain increased in intensity. If you have ever sprinted to find cover from the rain because it was coming down so hard you were about to be soaked, you will understand how hard I was running by the time I got back to the house. I sprinted up onto the back porch, tried to shake some water off myself, took off my wet shoes and stepped into the kitchen. When I looked out the window over the sink I realized it had completely stopped raining! I started laughing and said, "God, were you just spanking my rear end and telling me to get back in the house to pray?" To my knowledge, the only time it rained that day in Centralia was the two minutes that I went outside to take that early jog.

God used that "coincidence" to remind me of three principles from scripture: God can use the weather to serve His purposes. A good father disciplines his children; God is willing to discipline us. Prayer is part of the work in which God has called us to participate.

# A Timely Letter

I'd like to give credit to Vickie Spry for introducing me to the term 'God–Incidence.' One of the first incidents that she shared with me happened in the 2000s. Vickie has led a women's Bible study for a couple of decades. Her Monday night study has been an encouraging and learning time for many women over the years. In the early 2000s the group was using a curriculum called "Thin Within."

The group invited one of the staff members of the Thin Within ministry to come speak at one of their studies. The group was so encouraged by the speaker that during the following week's gathering, they all decided to write notes of encouragement to the staff person and send them together in a package. They wanted to thank her for the example of faith that she set and for the words she had shared.

A few weeks later, Vickie heard back from the staff member. She had received the package and told Vickie that it had come at the perfect time. After speaking at Harrisburg Christian Church, she had gone on vacation where she spent time reflecting on her involvement in the Thin Within ministry. She was feeling discouraged and was struggling with a decision about the future. As she came home from vacation she had decided to resign from the ministry.

When she read the letters in the package, she received the encouragement and words that she needed to realize that she was being effective in her role. She decided against resigning.

The Harrisburg group had no idea that the staff member was discouraged, but they were thankful to have been used by God. Writing letters just seemed like a kind gesture and a good idea, but God had much more in store for the group.

# Apology

I owed a man in our town an apology. On multiple occasions over the years, I have sensed a conviction from the Holy Spirit that I have been in the wrong in the way I've treated others. This was another one of those cases. I had participated in conversations that put this man in a bad light. I felt like God was telling me to go apologize. Apologies can be very difficult and awkward, and I thought the best way to apologize would be to do it in person.

The problem was that I didn't know where this man lived and I wasn't sure how I was going to go about contacting him. I was also sort of dragging my heels and embarrassed. If I asked someone else where this man lived, they might ask me why, and then I'd have to tell them my story, which I was already embarrassed about. I was under conviction which is also uncomfortable and so I wanted to get it over with as soon as I could.

It was in the fall when this occurred and I was teaching and coaching middle school football in Centralia. I went through the school day and then right to football practice. We were approaching the end of the season. As the last few minutes of practice came to a close, I looked over by the school building and guess who was standing there alone watching practice? The man to whom I needed to apologize. It was the first time I had seen him at a practice and he didn't have a son on the team. He just happened to be at his first practice on the day I was needing to give him an apology.

I swallowed my pride and went over and apologized as soon as practice ended. He was very gracious and received my apology. I think God had an assignment for me. I don't think it was a coincidence that he was there that day.

# Gut Feeling

The following incident and the "A Timely Letter" story happened the day I began writing the rough draft for this book sixteen years ago (yes, I know, it took a while to finish it). They are examples of how God orchestrates situations and times them perfectly.

A man came to interview as a worship leader candidate at First Baptist Church of Centralia. As part of the interview process he led the worship on Sunday morning at the church. I was phasing out of my role on the worship team in Centralia and transitioning over to Harrisburg Christian Church, so I was not directly involved in the hiring process, but I had spent some time with the candidate in practice preparing for the service.

As I left the worship service that morning I had a gut feeling about his candidacy. Comments he made sent up some red flags in my mind. I felt his plans and ministry goals were not a good fit for our church and would lead to discouragement on his part if he were to accept the position. I didn't know if I should initiate a conversation with the candidate or avoid trying to influence him since I was relocating to Harrisburg. I also didn't want to discourage him if Centralia was where God was leading him to be.

I discussed my thoughts with Kathleen and even used the words 'gut feeling' when I explained my thoughts. I prayed that God would lead and cause our paths to cross and let me know if I should say something to the candidate.

Before the evening service that night, there was a meal at the church. I saw the potential worship leader across the room. The gut feeling returned and I prayed again, "God, do I bring this up or remain silent?"

As I walked over to throw away my paper plate from the meal, the candidate walked up to me and said these exact words, "So, what is your gut feeling?" I took that comment as an assignment from God. I shared my concerns. He thanked me and ended up not taking the position.

# The Cross

Robert 'Doc' Kinkead, a retired veterinarian, was drenched in perspiration from the mid-August heat. He had just finished putting new skids under a mineral feeder and started to put away his tools, but God had an assignment for him.

Doc describes himself as a 'man of science.'

"Faith is something I cannot prove and it is hard to accept." In reflecting on the following incident he said, "I cannot explain or make sense of what occurred that day."

As Doc began to put away his tools he felt a very strange impulse. Though he had no plans to do another project when he walked into the barn, he knew in that moment he was going to construct a lighted cross to hang from the chimney on the south end of the Kinkead home. He and his wife Karen had not previously discussed the idea. It was not on a to-do list somewhere. It was an impulsive idea in every sense of the word.

Doc got right to work, and as he moved he felt an unseen presence helping—almost manipulating his actions. He looked over at the lumber supply. There were two 2 x 4s that proportionally made a cross that looked about the right size for the chimney. Doc didn't even measure them. The cross would need to be stable at the center joint. Right there in the scrap pile lay a ten inch square piece of three quarter inch plywood that would work. He screwed and bolted it together, again finding the right hardware there in the barn.

As Doc was admiring his work, the word "Lights!" came into his mind, like a shout in his head. He turned around and on the shelf in front of him was a dust-covered fifty foot light rope that the Kinkeads had purchased but hadn't used for Christmas decorations the previous year. It might have been tricky to attach the rope, but also on the shelf just happened to be a box of galvanized nails with larger than normal heads, perfect for nailing along the 2 x 4s and weaving the lighted rope through. After the weaving was done, the rope light was just the right size with only four inches extending beyond the frame.

Doc needed the framework necessary to support the cross against the chimney and the roof, and sure enough, laying in the scrap pile were two more 2 x 4s that were just the right size. Doc was able to construct the cross without ever plugging in a skill saw.

As Doc carried the cross toward the south side of the house, he said he felt a little like the man in the Bible who was pulled out of the crowd to carry the cross for Jesus. He found the ladder already on the south side of the house, left from a past project. He moved the ladder to the chimney, carried up the cross, and found that it fit with only two inches to spare on each side.

This project from God happened around 2008 and the cross hung for almost ten years. Even though it was not treated lumber, it never bowed or sagged during that time. Many people have been reminded of Jesus' sacrifice while driving past the Kinkead house on Route J, and Doc will always remember his assignment from God. Though Doc has no explanation for the way those moments made him feel, he has wondered "God, why me?" as he reflects on that day.

# The Gift of Teaching

I experience a God–Incidence on a weekly basis. I get an idea from God, and God uses me to help someone in the Harrisburg Christian Church congregation.

As I am preparing to teach or preach, I will have an idea come to mind. The idea usually fits into one or more of the following categories:

It might be a verse in the Bible that jumps out at me personally, causing me to think differently or make a change in my life that I can share as an example.

It might be a question I begin to ask myself or that I can ask the audience when I speak.

It might be an illustration, an analogy, or a visual aid that helps explain the concept I am trying to communicate.

It might be a way to apply the message to life.

After I get the idea, I incorporate it into the sermon or teaching and God uses it. One of the reasons I know God is using it is because people will often make comments to me like, "That was exactly what I needed to hear today." or "That message really spoke to me." I do not think it is a coincidence that I get these ideas popping into my head that help people who are wanting to follow God. I believe this is evidence of God at work!

My experience matches up with what the Bible teaches. According to the Bible, when a person becomes a Christian, the Holy Spirit dwells in them and then the Spirit equips that person with one or more spiritual gifts which gives them the capacity and desire to get assignments from God that will benefit other Christians. In my case, the Holy Spirit has given me the gift of teaching as described above.

Some have the gift of serving. Just like God gives me ideas to use for a message, He gives others nudges toward people they can serve. They will often hear how much their act of service helped.

Some have the gift of mercy. God gives them compassion for someone who is suffering and also gives them ideas of ways to comfort others. They will often hear how their presence really helped a person through a tough time.

What are some gifts that God has given you? As you grow in your capacity to hear from the Holy Spirit and respond in obedience, you will experience God–Incidences on a more regular basis. As you follow through on the Holy Spirit's leading you will discover that you are helping those who are wanting to follow God. One of our goals at Harrisburg Christian Church is to help people discover their gifts and use them to serve the Lord. If you do not currently have a church that you are connected to, I would like to encourage you to find one that will help you discover and use your gifts. It is exciting to experience the 'God assignments' that come from growing in your understanding of your gifts and how the Holy Spirit communicates.

# Chapter Five

## Does God Send Signs?

Something that is difficult to convey with words is the intensity of emotions that are birthed when these incidents take place. As people have recounted their stories to me, they still get emotional when they tell them. On multiple occasions I will hear the comment, "I get goosebumps just thinking about it."

God has a way of getting our attention through simple things like the words of a song, sermon, or a passing comment. Even a simple act of nature can be a message from God when it happens at the right moment. In the moment the incident takes place, it speaks deeply to us. Though it is hard to communicate through writing how powerfully these signs affected each person, they were deeply moved. Timing seems to be an essential element of God–Incidences.

I also think it is worth noting that the recipients of these signs immediately understood the message. It wasn't a situation where they considered a couple of possible meanings and picked one later. The message was very clear to them at the time of the incident. The incidents were attention grabbers that the recipient—and this author—recognized as signs from God. In "Redemption," I think the way the numbers lined up in Aaron's story was a sign of affirmation from God.

# Redemption

Aaron Vassar moved with his wife, MJ, to the Harrisburg community in 2018 to work at Coyote Hill Christian Children's Home. They began as relief parents and then transitioned to house parents at the first of the year.

Aaron had a tough childhood. He was abandoned by his mother as an infant. His aunt and grandmother took him into their home allowing him to stay out of the foster care system. But Aaron was difficult to raise. Seeking acceptance, he was continually drawn to the wrong crowd, and got involved in drug use and selling drugs. He was in and out of juvenile detention and later, jail.

In his mid twenties, Aaron met MJ and fell in love with her and her baby from a previous relationship. Aaron wanted to make a change. He remembered the positive impression he had of Christians from an early church experience. He decided to go back to church. He attended the church where MJ's parents were involved. In the worship service that day, Aaron heard the preacher say, "If you do what you've always done, you'll get what you've always gotten." He came home and said, "God, you can have me, but you're going to have to fix me, because I am a mess." Aaron picked up a Bible and began reading. He had read the Bible in prison, but this time it was different. Aaron describes it as seeming like this Bible was written in a new language. He began to highlight verses that were meaningful to him and he stayed up until three in the morning reading and discovering.

Aaron surrendered his life to the Lord and began to experience the power of Jesus, which gave him a new direction in life. His faith continued to grow and his old life continued to fade. By his late thirties he and MJ were applying to work in Christian service at Coyote Hill.

Unfortunately, Aaron's mother was unable to break away from the lifestyle she was in; before she died she had abandoned *eight children*. She died on *January 12th* at the age of *thirty-nine*.

God sent Aaron a message of encouragement, a sign, when on *January 12th,* 2019 at the age of *thirty-nine*, he moved into House 5 at Coyote Hill as a house parent. His new role would allow him and MJ to take into their home up to *eight children* who are abused, abandoned, or neglected.

Aaron's story is a reminder that not only can God change lives, but he can also take hardship from our past and bring good from it. Aaron's past hardship has given him a heart for children without parents able to care for them. The redeeming God is using Aaron's past for good.

# A Heavenly Hug

Within a year and a half, Doug and Joanna McDowell lost three of their four parents. Doug's mom died in December of 2017. Joanna's dad died in January of 2019. Then, in May of 2019, Doug's father was critically injured in an accident on I-70 while driving to Columbia from his Vandalia home.

William McDowell, also known as 'Doc' for his career as a veterinarian, had suffered a cervical spinal cord injury. He was placed on life support in the hospital's ICU. Because of a ventilator tube and William's inability to move his hands, communication was limited and difficult. William was communicating through eye blinks and subtle head movements and at times, he was difficult to read. The family continued to let William know how much he was loved and how thankful they were for him. They kept the room filled with hymns, prayers, and scriptures being read to comfort and support William's faith. Doug and his older brother, Jim, knew he would be dying soon. The two brothers would be responsible for the agonizing decision of when to remove life support.

William had retired from his veterinary practice. He cared for his wife Charlotte through a long battle with Parkinson's, and he maintained a small farm and a herd of cattle on their farm south of Vandalia, near Wellsville. During his time in the hospital, the family members were making trips to the farm to chore and check on things.

After about five days of being in the ICU, Doug went alone up to the farm to feed the cattle. His mind was filled with memories of his dad, the Christian faith of his family, and the lingering decision of when to remove life support. It had been an exhausting and emotionally draining week. Doug was grieving and praying and telling the Lord how much he was going to miss his dad.

In order to better understand the sign from God that Doug received, and how this sign was a unique fit for him, it would be helpful to know that Doug is fascinated by God's creation. His studies in exercise physiology have given him a deep appreciation for the human body and how intricate and detailed it is. He also loves being out in nature and enjoying the things God has made. Doug and his family have a deep Christian faith and also a love for music. He grew up playing instruments and singing around the living room. Doug is currently in a local band named the "Good Turn Daily Bluegrass Band."

As Doug was finishing putting grain in the calf feeder, he looked toward the east and there was a rainbow. He could see the full rainbow and even hints of a second. Doug immediately felt reassured that God keeps His promises, including the promise that those who believe receive eternal life and that for Christians, death is not a goodbye forever, simply a goodbye for now.

The Bible points to the rainbow as a sign that God keeps His promises. In the book of Genesis, God told Noah that the rainbow would be a sign of His promise never again to destroy mankind by a flood. Doug began to ponder other promises in the Bible, like when Jesus said, "I am the resurrection and the life. The one who believes in me will live, even though he dies." (John 11:25)

Doug decided to drive over to the cemetery where his mother's grave was and where he soon would be burying his father. His radio was tuned to 88.3 KJAB, a local Christian radio station that plays southern and bluegrass gospel. The rainbow lingered, and at one time Doug pulled over and took a picture of it. When he got near the cemetery, he pulled his vehicle over at an angle where he could see the end of the rainbow lining up directly with his mother's gravestone. He paused there for a moment and then began to drive closer to the grave site. As Doug pulled up to the grave, the following lyrics came on his radio:

"You may not have the answers to the questions in your life. And you and I may never know all the reasons why. You feel you've been forsaken. If someone only knew. If someone only understood, just what you're going through. God knows, and God cares. He holds the answers to all your prayers. God knows, and God cares. He gave His only Son to die on the cross so you and I would know, that God knows..." ("God Knows" by The Kingsmen).

Tears filled Doug's eyes as the song continued to play and the rainbow continued to shine (it shone for at least fifteen minutes). To find a song that Doug doesn't already know is a pretty rare occurrence because of his musical background, but it was the first time Doug had ever heard this song. God comforted Doug's soul that afternoon using the beauty of the rainbow, the promises of Jesus, and a gospel song that seemed written for just that moment. Doug describes the incident as feeling like he was getting a 'Heavenly Hug' from the Lord.

William passed away two days later on May 23rd. He is buried next to Charlotte.

# Broken Love

*Written by Jean Japko*

God's presence is around us, but are we aware of it? If we are aware of it, do we act on His presence or ignore it? We may not ignore it on purpose, it could be that we can't believe he is talking to us in this manner.

I had an experience while I was going through a difficult time. I saw a sign from God, which helped direct my life for the better. I had been married for almost ten years when I decided to leave my abusive husband. It was a very hard decision. Divorce wasn't common in our family—we were taught to work through difficult situations. I didn't think I could face ten more years being with this sadness.

Through many tears and prayers I got an answer. I still remember my experience like it was yesterday. I had just gotten done with exercise and was sitting in my car. I was praying to God to give me a sign that this was the correct decision and it was okay to leave my marriage. I was wiping away my tears and had looked up at the windshield. There it was...my sign. My answer to my prayers, I couldn't believe it. All I know is that at that time there was a sense of peace that came over me and I knew it was from God. What was the sign you ask? The windshield was clear and dry except for an area with condensation. The condensation was shaped into a perfect heart, but it was upside down. To me that was a sign from God. He had provided the sign to show me my marriage was not a healthy, good marriage but one of a broken love—that this type of love is not correct.

At that moment a sense of relief, calmness and peace came over me. Yes, it was the correct decision to proceed with the divorce. If I had ignored that sign, I may still be in an unhappy and dangerous place. Since I looked at that sign as being from God I have a much better life. For this I thank God.

# Comfort to Parents

Kathleen was in tears over a parenting issue that had happened one day. With the kids finally in bed, she was sharing the story with me in our Centralia home. I didn't have many comforting words to say, nor did I know how to pray, but we discussed the issue and then went around as usual and prayed for our children in their beds before we went to sleep.

At this time in our marriage, Kathleen and I were in the habit of reading a short devotional together in the morning before getting out of bed. I wake up quicker, so I was the one who would read. The following morning I grabbed the book, *The Power of a Praying Husband* by Stormie Omartian, off my night stand. I opened the book to where my bookmark was and discovered that the prayer on the page fit perfectly with the situation we were wrestling with the night before. My original intention was to pray over Kathleen silently, but once I read the prayer, I prayed it out loud.

The theme of the prayer got Kathleen's attention "What chapter was that!?" Kathleen asked after I said 'amen.' We both knew that prayer was exactly what we needed.

Too many times to count, we have had comments, songs, sermons, Bible verses, "jump out at us" and meet the needs of our heart or answer questions that we were pondering. Again, I think it would be a mistake to consider all these incidents coincidence. I think God is behind many of them, using the media and people around us to give us encouragement and counsel.

# A Reassuring Song

Caring for elderly family members is a value I have come to appreciate and understand more from examples set by members of the Harrisburg community. Herb and Judy Owens were one of the couples that demonstrated this value to me.

Judy's mother, Ila Mae Long, was a widow when I first moved to Harrisburg. At that time, Illa Mae was living independently at home. Family members would stop by and check in on her and give her rides to church and other community events. One of my early memories of Illa Mae is watching her sit in her grandson's roofless truck as they spun through a deep hole at a mud run organized by a group of guys with souped-up trucks. Very soon after my arrival to Harrisburg, Illa Mae's health and physical and mental abilities began to decline.

Soon the family members were needing to stop by more regularly. Eventually Illa Mae moved into Herb and Judy's home. As Herb and Judy transitioned and retired from their jobs in Columbia, caring for Illa Mae became a full-time task. She loved coming to Harrisburg Christian Church and for a while, Herb was able to bring her in a wheelchair until she became completely homebound. After years of care, the day finally came when Illa Mae went home to be with the Lord.

I got the call from Herb and Judy and went out to their house to try and provide comfort and talk with them about the funeral. When I arrived, they shared with me a comforting God–Incidence that they had just received from the Lord.

After Illa Mae's body had been taken from the house, Herb, Judy and their daughter Charlyn, were sitting in the living room. As they were sitting, music started to play. The sound was coming from a toy box in the corner of the room. Judy got up to see where the music was coming from. In the toy box she found a children's book that had the lyrics to different hymns and an assortment of buttons down the side of the book. The buttons could be pressed to select a song to play while a person was reading or singing with the words in the book. Judy held the book and listened to the tune that was playing. It was "What a Friend We Have in Jesus." The tune 'just happened' to be Illa Mae's favorite hymn.

As I walked into the living room later, there was appropriate grieving, but also an expression of faith from the family. They had received the spontaneous song as a reassurance from the Lord of His love for them and His care for their departed loved one.

# A Light in the Dark

When you first get to know Reggie Wilhite, it becomes quickly evident that she has been given a kind and soft heart for both people and animals. She doesn't turn away hurting or needy people and she doesn't turn away a stray animal. At the time of this writing she was housing four cats, none of which she went looking for; they found her.

The late 1980s were tumultuous years for Reggie and her girls who were approaching their middle school years. Reggie had begun a new marriage that unexpectedly created a blended family situation. Her husband's teenage children asked to move in with their dad and join his new wife and family.

In addition to the new people inside the house, there were new animals outside the house. The family's rural location on Route E, their popular Basset Beagle Hound, and Reggie's soft heart increased the frequency by which the local strays and free-roaming dogs would stop by. Some began to call it home. When one of the strays went into heat, Reggie's load began to feel too heavy to carry.

The pressure had been building. Reggie was working full-time at Boone County Bank, serving at Harrisburg Christian Church, working on a new marriage, raising two girls, navigating the dynamics of older kids in the house, and being an unexpected step-mom. The dog in heat was attracting more attention than normal from the roaming dogs in the neighborhood. It really wasn't a good time for another litter of pups.

There was a pen for the dog in the backyard but the gate was difficult to operate. The latches did not always cooperate. Reggie put the adopted stray in the pen for the night and headed to bed. Maybe a good night's sleep would help ease the pressure for everyone.

But sleep was not to be had. Reggie was awakened in the middle of the night by a group of dogs in her yard that were creating a ruckus. It sounded like the gate had come unlatched and the stray was getting some unwanted attention. As Reggie groggily got out of bed, she was hit with another wave of emotion. She was feeling overwhelmed, stressed, and trapped. It seemed like nothing had been going right lately. Life had gotten extremely difficult.

Reggie stumbled outside. The gate on the pen was hard enough to operate in the daytime, but now in the yard without a dusk to dawn light, flashlight, or her glasses, it would be a 'miracle' if she could get it latched. As Reggie rounded the corner of the house, she saw a glow coming from the pen. She looked up in the sky. It was a clear night, the moon and stars were visible, but the glow was brighter than what the night sky could produce. She walked up to the gate. With her progressive lense glasses still back in the house, she had unexpected visual clarity. She reached down to the dog pen door and latched it easily. All the dogs settled down.

In that moment a peace came over Reggie. It was the first bright spot (literally) in Reggie's life in many weeks and she sensed God's presence and the Lord communicating to her that everything was going to be fine. She walked back to the house with a sense of relief. She realized that her situation wasn't going to be fixed immediately, but that God hadn't lost sight of what was going on. The sign from God was a special moment of timely peace that Reggie will always treasure.

# I Remember

The first time I had a conversation with Billy Curtis, he spoke first saying, "I want you to baptize me."

I think Billy and I had probably exchanged greetings in the past. I coached and baptized his grandson. His wife, Susan, had become a regular at Harrisburg Christian Church, but when Billy made his first visit to a Sunday morning worship service, God was prompting him to begin a new life with Jesus at the center.

We set up a time to meet Sunday afternoon. I didn't know what to expect when I met with Billy. He is a big, bearded, direct man and I was initially a little intimidated by him. But as he shared his story with me at the kitchen table in his home on Route E, I began to discover that Billy's lack of church attendance over the years was not an indication of a lack of belief in God. Two incidents that had occurred in his past were deeply implanted in his soul.

Billy and his siblings had gathered in their mother Leena's hospital room to be with her in her final hours before she passed. She was about to lose her battle with cancer and the doctors had called the family in. Around dinner time, Billy offered to stay in the room while the rest of the family went to grab something to eat. Billy was only alone with her a few minutes when her breathing changed. Leena took a big final breath, exhaled and didn't breathe again. At the very moment of that final breath, Billy watched the lights in the room get bright. It was as if there was a power surge going on.

As Billy pondered the light and looked at his mother, the closed door to the room opened and shut. Billy looked over at the door thinking one of his siblings must have walked in. Seeing that they had not come into the room, he thought they must be in the hall, so he went to the door to let them know that Mom had taken her final breath. When he opened up the door, he found the hallway empty.

Billy had been told of an unseen spiritual reality, that there is life after death and that our soul continues after our body dies. As he sat in the hospital room and looked at his mother's body, he was convinced that something unseen and immaterial had moved through the room at her death.

A few years later Billy again found himself in a hospital room. This time with his father, Paul, in an emergency situation. Paul, a long time alcoholic, had gotten drunk on whiskey and suffered a heart attack. Billy watched his father 'die' three times on the table, each time his heart was shocked back to life by the emergency personnel. Billy watched his father's three hundred pound body rise almost airborn from the electrical jolts.

Paul was placed on life support and the doctor called the family in; he wasn't going to last long. There was major damage to the lower part of his heart. After the second day on life support the doctor informed the family that Paul wouldn't make it through the night.

That evening Billy was in the room with his Uncle Everett, a preacher. Everett was unique in his training as a teacher of the Bible. Though Billy didn't know it at the time, his uncle was illiterate. He learned the Bible by listening to tapes and having his wife read to him. Even though he held a Bible when he would preach, even opening up to the marked pages, he would not read the scripture. Instead his wife helped him memorize it ahead of time. God had used Uncle Everett to lead many people to the Lord and now he was going to use him to expose Billy to the spiritual realm.

As Billy began to think about his father and the news from the doctor, he began to weep. Uncle Everett spoke up, "What are you crying for? Your dad's going home."

Billy looked at his Uncle with tears in his eyes and said, "You heard the doctor, he's not going to make it through the night."

"Didn't you hear that angel?" Uncle Everett argued as he pointed to the corner of the room.

Billy looked at his uncle with skepticism.

"You can't see that angel?" Everett exclaimed. "That angel over there just said that your dad is going home."

"But he's on life support!" Billy replied.

"That angel said you're father is going home and that is what is going to happen," concluded Uncle Everett. At that moment Billy had a physical sensation that he had never had before and has never had since. The hair on his right arm stood straight up and what felt like a flow of electricity went up his right arm, across his shoulders and down his left arm. Billy never saw an angel, but he felt something unique. He also got surprising news the next day.

Paul made it through the night and when the doctor made his morning rounds he explained to the family, "I don't know what happened. I'd like to monitor him for a few days, just to make sure, but it looks like he may be going home."

Paul did go home, he lived another five and a half years. He stopped drinking, stopped smoking, got baptized, and started going to church. Billy saw his father change and the prediction from the angel come to pass.

As Billy and I spoke at the kitchen table, I realized that God had been revealing himself to Billy over the years and planting faith in his heart for a long time.

81

That day, September 2nd, 2018, both Billy and Susan acknowledged their desire to trust Jesus as their Savior and surrender their lives to him. They were baptized the next day at Harrisburg Christian Church.

# Chapter Six

## Does God Change People?

There is an expression in our community that people use when someone does the same hurtful, sinful, or dumb action again and again. "Some people never change." There is a sense of hopelessness and fatalism in this comment.

If you've ever wondered if there is hope for change in your life or the lives of people you care about, I have good news. God changes people.

The following story is mine, but I could point you to hundreds of people that I know personally who have similar stories of God changing them. The previous "I Remember" story was one of them. I believe that the most prevalent God–Incidence on the planet is that when a person trusts Jesus as their Savior and Lord, their life 'just happens' to begin to change. God changes them from the inside out. It is happening not only in Boone County, but all over the world.

# Born Again

I was raised in a God-fearing home. We attended church every Sunday and I am thankful for the opportunities my parents gave me and my siblings to learn about God. Though I was being brought up in a religious culture, I began to become neutral about God. During my Sophomore year in high school some of my friends heard a rumor that the public library had a copy of *The Satanic Bible* by Anton Szandor LaVey. They were talking around the lunch table about going to look at it after school. I spoke up and said, "Look guys, I'm no Jesus freak, but I'm not messing with Satan." That was a good summary of my attitude toward God at the time. I didn't want to put him first in my life, but I didn't want to swing to the side of evil, either.

At the time, I was also drifting into the partying scene with my friends. I began to participate in activities that at first I felt guilty about doing, but after a while my conscience seemed to develop some calluses and I began to participate with few reservations. I was also becoming more of a 'user of people.' If you could do something for me, I'd be friendly to you. If you didn't have anything to offer, I didn't have much time for you. I was living a self-centered life.

During my Junior year in high school, a new teacher/coach moved in. Mr. Mark Mundell was a chiseled former NAIA (National Association of Intercollegiate Athletics) national championship winning football offensive guard. He moved back to Brookfield, Missouri to take his first teaching job as a Biology teacher and football and wrestling coach.

I was a sports fan and in awe of this new teacher who had a recent conversation with the San Francisco 49ers about playing Pro, only to be told that he was too small.

Rumor had it that Mark was interested in starting an FCA group (Fellowship of Chrisitan Athletes). I thought, "I go to church, and I like sports, sounds like a good group for me." I offered to host the first meeting at my home and FCA began at Brookfield in 1985. That year, the FCA leaders hosted a New Year's Eve lock-in for the high school students. We packed into the basement of a bank with snacks and movies to last the night. Some of my friends showed up high. They had their first experience with a 'water bong' and they were telling me about it. Had I not been helping set up for the lock-in, I probably would have been right there with them.

Amidst *Rocky* movies and other movie titles from the eighties, the FCA leaders showed a movie titled *A Thief in the Night*. Similar to the more modern *Left Behind* movie, this sixties hippie movie depicted characters with long sideburns and bell bottoms, and told the story of a group of people who are left on earth after the rapture (an event some Christians believe will take place before the second coming of Jesus where all the Christians will be taken from the earth).

As I watched the movie that night, I realized that although I had been to church all my life, I had never placed my trust in Jesus as my savior or surrendered my life to Him. I realized that I was heading to Hell and separation from God and I was sensing a deep conviction to make a change.

When I got home the next morning, I went into my bathroom where I could be alone and I prayed a prayer like I saw the woman in the movie pray. I don't remember the exact words, but it went something like: "Jesus I know that I am a sinner, I believe you died on the cross for my sins and I want to accept you as my Savior and Lord." After I prayed, I waited for a 'peace' to come over me because that is what happened to the lady in the movie. I didn't feel a peace, so I prayed the prayer again. Still no peace. At that point, I didn't know what else to do and I was tired, so I went to sleep.

Though there were no lightning bolt moments in the morning, after that day my life began to move in a new direction. I no longer was neutral about God, I began to read my Bible, attend Bible studies and FCA. I continued to go to church, but now it was different; I was more interested in what was going on.

In the areas where I had developed calluses on my conscience, it felt like my conscience had woken back up. I began to feel guilty about the way I was living my life. I wasn't comfortable doing the activities I had done in the past and I began to pull away from them. I also experienced a new desire to serve people instead of using people. I began to have a desire that still exists today to help others even if they can't do anything for me. I also developed the desire to tell others about Jesus and what He had done for me and what He could do for them.

God is changing me into a different person. I have seen Him do this in hundreds of people's lives over the years. In the Bible, Jesus spoke about being "born again." This born again experience commonly occurs when the following things happen: People hear about the love that God has for them. They sense some sort of calling or conviction from God. They acknowledge that they are sinful and in need of forgiveness. They realize that God sent His Son, Jesus to die in their place as a substitute to pay the penalty for their sins and that after dying He demonstrated His power by rising from the dead. They trust that Jesus is their Savior and surrender their lives to Him. Following these events, people's lives begin to change. It happened to me, just as it has happened to many others I know. I do not think it is just a coincidence that these beliefs about God are so tied to the changing of lives. It is more than a coincidence, it is a God–Incidence. If you are reading this and feeling an inner conviction or calling from God, I want to encourage you to respond. Trust Jesus as your Savior and surrender your life to Him. He is still changing people.

# Chapter Seven

## Does God Rescue People?

The Bible is filled with God stories. There are stories recorded in the Bible of God preventing people from being burned, or mangled by lions, or from being harmed by a poisonous snake bite. The following stories may not be quite as dramatic as some of the Bible stories, but they certainly got the attention of those involved. The Bible implies that there are angels who serve us and at times may protect us. I would like to present these stories as local examples of rescues by the hand of God directly or by angels.

# A Miracle Catch

Roy Boyer makes his living climbing up telephone poles. His tall, athletic build is perfect for the task. For fourteen years he has strapped over sixty pounds of equipment to his waist, free climbed telephone poles, secured himself with safety straps, and hooked up fiber optic wires around the country. His experience, training, and caution had allowed him to be accident free all fourteen years up until March 12th of 2019, in southern Mississippi.

Maybe it was fatigue, it was the last pole of the day and the fourth in a row in which Roy was taking the climbing role for the crew. Maybe it was the frustrating text that he had just read that had distracted his focus. Maybe it was the pole. The harder poles in southern Mississippi have a slightly different wood and treatment than the Missouri poles that Roy typically climbs. They also have a steel ground wire with very little give as opposed to the copper wires in Missouri. Whatever the reason, Roy was thirty feet up a fifty foot pole when his left gaff (steel claw on the side of his climbing boot) made contact with the ground wire instead of the pole and his foot abruptly slipped over two feet down the pole. His right leg was caught off guard and couldn't hold the weight of his body and equipment. He began plummeting to the ground below.

Roy saw the ground coming fast. Because of the way he had slipped, he was falling in a sitting position. As Roy braced himself for contact, he felt two arms underneath his. The helping arms allowed his body positioning to change, straightening his legs. His left heel hit the ground first. Roy later found out that it had been shattered into eight pieces. The rest of his body felt like it was being gently lifted up and laid on the ground.

When Roy came to, the six other men on his crew were surrounding him asking if he was okay. It took a bit for Roy to come out of his state of shock. The men helped him get his equipment off, get to the truck, and to the local emergency room where X-rays confirmed his broken foot. Later that night Roy was released to go back to the hotel. The crew was cooking outside and retelling the story of the day. Roy spoke up and said, "Who ran over and caught me when I fell?" The men looked at him quizzically and Roy repeated the question and expanded a little on his experience of having helping hands underneath him. "Dude, nobody was around you!" was the crew's response.

Roy's memory of the event led him to believe that though a crew member was not there to catch him, he was caught by unseen hands. "I was caught by my guardian angel," Roy explained.

As of September 2019, Roy has seen his mobility increase. He was walking in a boot by July, without a boot in August and he began physical therapy to further rehabilitate.

As a father/guardian to three children in his home, he looks back to what could have been a death fall and believes that one of the reasons God saved him was because of his three kids. On August 4th, Harrisburg Christian Church celebrated the baptism of two of those kids. Roy is giving God the glory and hoping to get back to climbing in the future.

# Mountain Rescue

Cal Clark loves the outdoors. His primary residence is on Route E near Harrisburg, but because of his love for the outdoors, he built a cabin "off the grid" in the Colorado wilderness. Cal has spent time hunting all sorts of game. He also serves as a guide for elk, bear, and turkey hunters.

His heart lit up when his oldest daughter Anna began to show an interest in hunting at an early age. As she grew, they spent a lot of time in the woods, and their trophies of deer and a black bear showcase their successes.

During Anna's Senior year in high school, they set aside a week to head to Colorado for Anna's first elk hunt. The future homecoming queen set down her school books and grabbed a .308 bolt-action Savage rifle. She and her father headed out to the rough South Fork, Colorado terrain for a week long October hunt. In addition to her hunting skills, Anna is an accomplished equestrian. She and Cal used mules the first few days to get to remote places where they could find elk. After day three of no elk sightings, Cal decided to try a different tactic.

For their evening hunt, they loaded up their guns and gear to look in a different area that was accessible by four-wheelers. Cal's friend and local resident, Billy Dilly (yes, that's his real name), took the lead up the steep and obstacle filled mountain trail. Anna was in the middle followed by Cal. Climbing a mountain in four-wheelers is not an easy task.

Anna had ridden plenty on the four-wheelers at their home in Missouri, but riding in the mountains was a whole different game.

This hunting trip had been different for Cal. Through the years he had been on many different hunts both as a guide and a hunter, and he knew there were very real risks. Cal had seen accidents caused by slick spots, ice, snow, unstable terrain, and exposure to the cold over the years. Now it was his daughter on the trip and his protective instincts were heightened. He was determined not to let his guard down. He also sensed that his own ability to protect was not adequate. When recalling the story, he stated, "I wanted more than what I could do and I was afraid that something out of my control would happen."

Cal's prayers had increased as a result. He found himself throughout the day throwing up brief prayers to God. "Lord, look out for us," "Keep an eye on us," "Keep us safe." As he watched his daughter struggling with the four-wheeler and the trail in front of him, Cal continued to pray. He also started to get worried by what he was seeing.

Anna had been a little apprehensive that morning about the four-wheeler trip. She was much more comfortable on a mule than on a machine and Cal could see that she was having a hard time maneuvering the vehicle. The road they were on was steep, with areas of loose gravel and uneven ruts. Billy went around a root wad, over some ruts and up a steep incline. Cal watched Anna's vehicle rock off center for a moment on one of the ruts. The rear wheel of her four-wheeler came off the ground just as she increased the throttle. When the wheel made contact, instead of spinning out, it caught firm ground, thrusting the four-wheeler quickly up the steep bank and over backwards on Anna.

Cal watched helplessly as his daughter fell from her seat. The full sized four-wheeler slammed directly on her and bounced off to the side. It looked like the handle bar area had landed directly on Anna's head and neck area, and for a moment, her body was completely hidden by the ATV above her before the momentum of the crash rolled it off. Sprinting to where Anna lay, he feared the worse. Cal had no doubt that she was hurt badly; he just hoped she was alive.

And then, Anna stood up. Amidst the relief of seeing her on her feet, the first thing that came to Cal's mind was "God, you answered my prayers!" Reaching his daughter, he found her shook up. Anna said her back was hurting a little. She was scared, but after resting for a bit, Anna was ready to continue the hunt. This time she rode on the back of her dad's four-wheeler.

Thankfully, the rest of the trip was less eventful. They did not come back with an elk, but Cal came back with a story of God's hand of protection during their trip. He believes there was divine help that afternoon and thanks God for answering his prayers.

# The Helping Hand

Gabe Gilpin is a jack of all trades: construction, auto mechanics, fireplaces, shower doors, small farming, and motorcycles. On cool fall days, he and his daring fiancée Jodi would load up on a motorcycle and hit the hilly curvy roads of the Boone County area. Over time, Jodi decided that she wanted to start riding her own bike. After Gabe purchased a blue and silver 2003 Suzuki 800 Intruder Volusia, Jodi began learning on their older and smaller black 1987 Suzuki 700 Intruder.

Jodi grew in her skills and it was time for a longer ride. The two grabbed their friend Jeff Sapp and headed to Route Y just outside of Ashland. Jeff was in the lead, followed by Jodi and then Gabe. As Gabe watched her taking the curves, he began to get nervous, she was coming into them too tight. "I've got to tell her to start on the outside." Gabe thought. As he was thinking this, they went down a hill with a curve at the bottom. Jodi was going into the curve too fast. Gabe saw it coming, but it was too late to warn her.

In agony, he watched as Jodi drifted off the road and into the ditch. The ditch was not just a grassy landing, there were rocks and a huge boulder ahead. As she went down into the ditch, her front tire hit a rock and bounced the front tire of her Intruder into a high back flip. The motorcycle and Jodi did a complete flip together and as the bike started to make the second rotation, Jodi let go.

Both the bike and Jodi were suspended in mid air getting ready to smash into the boulder. The bike was right above Jodi. Four hundred pounds of bike was about to crash on top of her and smash her into the rock. Then Gabe saw something he will never forget. Jodi's body stopped in mid-air. It was as if someone had grabbed her leather jacket and jerked her back. The motorcycle continued on its trajectory and slammed into the rock, smashing the bike.

Redirected, Jodi scraped along the ground. Gabe watched her stand right up, spin around and fall back down like a man getting shot in an old western movie. Amazingly, she walked away, bruised, shook up, and scratched up, but alive and not crushed. Gabe's aunt 'just happened' to be driving the first car to come on the scene and was able to take Jodi to her father-in-law who took her to the hospital where it was verified that she had no broken bones. Seven days later, Jodi attended her wedding shower with her arm in a sling and a thankful heart. She and Gabe were married that year and now have two amazing kids. Gabe continues to celebrate the day he saw the hand of God save his wife.

# A Water Rescue

Herb Owens was about to drown. He and his friend had returned to a familiar swimming hole in the Neosho area. It had been raining a lot recently and Shoal Creek was running a little faster than normal but the water level was on it's way down and seemed safe. The swimming hole area was at the base of a six to eight foot man-made waterfall. A concrete wall had been constructed to create a low water dam next to a pump house on the upper bank. Herb and his buddy liked to jump from the top of the wall into the pool of water below. Wisely, nineteen-year-old Herb suggested they check the dark pool of water for any logs or debris before jumping in.

The two friends walked down to the gravel bar at the base of the dam and Herb waded out toward the deep area near the concrete wall. The aging wall had developed some handholds throughout the years and swimmers could climb up the side of the wall through the falling water, get on the top ledge, and jump back in. The water quickly got too deep for wading and Herb swam the remaining ten to fifteen feet to the wall of the dam. When he reached the wall, he realized that the water was coming down too strongly for him to climb up. Herb turned around and began swimming back to shallow water but soon discovered that he was not making any progress. The back current created by the falling water from the dam was keeping Herb in the deep water.

Herb yelled for help, but his friend assumed he was only joking; the area looked fine from shore and he knew that Herb was a good swimmer. Surely he was just messing around. Herb's struggle and call for help did however, catch the attention of a water department maintenance worker who was by the pump house and he began to come down to the rock bar where Herb's friend stood. As Herb continued to struggle against the current, he became exhausted and disoriented and couldn't tell if he was above the water or under it. He began to breath in water and was on his way to drowning. As Herb was losing consciousness, he heard a very peaceful and calming voice that said to him, "Do not worry, you will be alright." Herb disappeared in the dark water and would not regain his consciousness until later that day in the hospital.

The situation above water was anything but peaceful. The maintenance worker who had responded to Herb's call saw him go under and began wading out to him. The problem was, he didn't know how to swim and so he paused in the waist deep water looking for a sign of Herb. Herb's friend was now scanning the dark pool as well. The situation had become critical, but there was no sign of Herb. And then, the maintenance worker felt something brush his leg. He reached down into the dark water and grabbed ahold of Herb's arm. Somehow, Herb had drifted over to the shallow area right up to the worker.

The worker 'happened' to know CPR and was equipped to perform what was needed to save Herb's life. They called for an ambulance. Herb awoke in the hospital thankful that, as the voice had assured him, he was going to be alright. Herb gives credit to God for the rescue. The calming voice, the worker being there, and his unconscious body drifting through the dark water to the exact place needed for rescue. A God–Incidence he will never forget.

# Help in the Fire

It was a regular night for the Skinner family. They had dinner, spent some evening time together, and then Mark and Dawn put their son Wesley down for bed before heading out to work on projects. Wesley, soon to be eleven years old, always went right to sleep, which gave his parents some evening project time out in the detached garage, located about forty feet from the house.

The night's task was repainting a serving tray and Dawn was priming it with Kilz. After about twenty minutes of work, Mark sniffed the air and asked Dawn, "Do you smell smoke?"

"You're probably just smelling this Kilz." Dawn replied. They both went back to work and then a few minutes later, the lights in the garage went out. That got their attention and they quickly headed to the house.

Opening the door, they found the house was full of smoke. Mark told Dawn to go upstairs and get Wesley and he'd find out what was going on. Dawn rushed up to the second story into Wesley's bedroom. The whole second floor was filled with smoke from floor to ceiling. Frantically she began to scream for Wesley, crawling around on the floor, sweeping with her arms and legs around the rooms and hall.

Needing air, Dawn opened a couple of windows and kicked out the screens and yelled down to Mark that she could not find Wesley. Mark immediately came up and started looking. After several minutes, there was still no contact with Wesley.

Mark and Dawn were now in danger from the smoke. They rushed down to the first floor for a quick breath and knew Wesley didn't have much time left. "We've got to get him this time," Mark said and they both headed back up.

Racing again up to the second floor they continued to look for Wesley, sweeping with their arms and praying. Mark yelled out as loud as he could, "Wesley!" In the moment that followed, Mark heard a faint sound. It seemed to originate from inside his head. He followed the direction of the sound and was led straight to the master bedroom closet where he discovered his son lying lifeless on the floor. He yelled at Dawn and carried Wesley out to the front yard. As Dawn called 911, Mark began CPR.

Of all the advantages of country living, being close to emergency workers is not one of them. Though they could hear sirens in the distance, it was going to be a while before emergency personnel would get down Devil's Washboard Road and find the Skinner's cabin.

When Mark first laid Wesley in the grass, he was lifeless. He wasn't breathing and there was no pulse. Mark had been doing CPR for about five to ten minutes, but it felt like an eternity as he looked at the body of his son. A couple of times it appeared that Wesley was going to take breaths on his own, but each time his breathing stopped. Still no pulse or breathing. Mark screamed a prayer in desperation, "God, you've got to help me!"

He gave his son one more rescue breath; Wesley came to. He began to breathe and started vomiting up black stuff from his mouth. When the emergency personnel arrived, Wesley was breathing, but still unconscious. Smoke continued to pour out of the house. A first floor refrigerator was the culprit of the fire. Smoke from the electrical short behind the fridge and the smoldering wood wall behind the plug was producing all the smoke. Wesley was taken in the Staff for Life helicopter to the University Hospital. He was treated and eventually made a full recovery.

The Skinners were overwhelmed by the response and help they received from the community and Perche Baptist Church as they recovered and repaired their home. At one point Mark stood up during the church announcements and told the congregation they could stop. They had all they needed, especially with a healthy son sitting next to them. The Skinners saw the hand of God at work in multiple ways, but point out three specifics as they share their story.

1. According to the Fire Marshall's comments to Mark after investigating, there was no reason for the garage lights to have gone off. The breaker was still on, but it was the loss of light that alerted the Skinners to the fire.

2. The noise that drew Mark's attention to the closet could have been from Wesley, but based on the condition of his body when Mark found him, he suspects the noise was aid from a heavenly source.

3. Following the 'screaming prayer,' Wesley began breathing. Mark and Dawn believe this was a direct answer to prayer.

Twelve years later, the Skinners continue to thank God for their thriving and healthy son.

# Tight Curves

Ray Cochran often gives credit to his praying mother. Although God's involvement in his story was not as clear to him at the time it happened, he suspects a divine hand was involved as he looks back. I wonder how many times his mother, Isabelle, prayed for safety as her sixteen-year-old son got his license and was given the keys to the family car.

Ray was spending part of his summer on a hay crew with some other Harrisburg teens. One evening after pulling into town from a day of picking up square bales of hay around the neighboring fields, the worn out crew decided to head out for a soda and some snacks. Ray happened to have the keys to the family's recent vehicle purchase, the nicest car the Cochrans had owned up to this point. It was a 1959 Chevy with a six cylinder motor and a "three on the tree" gear shift on the steering column. More power than Ray needed, but big enough to hold the whole hay crew.

The guys piled into the Chevy and headed east on Highway 124 to the Lakeside Store about five miles out of town. After purchases of various sodas and snacks with their hay money, the teens loaded back into the car. Ray was driving with a soda between his legs on the seat, his snack in one hand and the steering wheel in the other, adjusting his hands and snack as needed to shift. It was the perfect storm: the parent's car with too much power for a new driver, a sixteen-year-old at the wheel, night time, the group of teenage guys in the car to impress, trying to shift gears without spilling a drink or losing a snack, and the hilly curvy roads of Highway 124 with no shoulder.

Ray remembers coming to the S-curves right past the Route YY turn off. As he approached the last curve, he knew he was coming into it too fast. *We're going over,* Ray thought to himself. He hung onto the steering wheel, turned with the curve and prepared to head off into the ditch. To Ray's surprise, the tires held. They made the curve and made it back to Harrisburg.

The sixteen-year-old Ray interpreted this event as "skilled driving on his part." The seventy-five year-old Ray looks back at this night and credits the Lord for keeping them on the road. As far as Ray can remember, there was no mysterious turning of the steering wheel from an outside force, but the surprise of not going off the road has stuck with Ray for almost sixty years. As I listened to Ray's story, I wondered how many times the Lord has intervened in my life without me realizing it at the time.

# Chapter Eight

## What Counts?

Many stories were left out of this book. It is my hope that there will be a need for a sequel. Usually when I share these stories with others, they respond by telling me a story that happened to them. I hope the distribution of this book will create more conversations of God–Incidences in Boone County.

I intentionally left out stories about deceased loved ones communicating with the living. I did this for several reasons, but have had a number of people tell me stories over the years that would fit in that genre. Perhaps that will be a section in a future book.

I also intentionally left out stories of people meeting a spouse or a close friend and how those 'chance' meetings turned into a lifetime friendship or marriage. I feel the same way about connecting with Kathleen—she seemed God-sent. But I stayed away from love stories, even though many have been shared with me over the years and I can see the God–Incidences in them.

When you are writing a book on God–Incidences, you tend to notice them more. We just purchased a Jeep Patriot. I'm not much of a vehicle guy, nor am I very observant, but since purchasing a Patriot, I am seeing them everywhere.

Sometimes you are just more attuned to looking for specific things. I still don't think that every coincidence is a God–Incidence.

For example; on the first day of my sabbatical (the time Harrisburg Christian Church gave me to rest, refocus on the Lord, and write this book), Kathleen and I were traveling to Colorado to be coached and encouraged by our friends at Big Horn Ministries. We visited Kathleen's mother in Saint Joseph along the way.

The next day we were getting close to our destination and made one final dinner stop at Taco Bell. The young man taking our order was friendly and appeared to be in training. He asked how we were doing.

I mentioned that it had been a long day, that we had driven from Missouri. "Wow!" the man said. "That's a long trip. I've got a grandma who lives in Missouri—it's like Jesse James's hometown."

Kathleen asked, "Is she from Saint Joseph?"

"Yeh! That's it," he said.

My wife explained Saint Joseph was her hometown and that we had been there just that morning. We explained we were headed west on the first day of my sabbatical from pastoring in Missouri. The young man then told us his dad had just begun a three month sabbatical from their local Evangelical Free Church.

This was one of those conversations that leave you thinking, "What are the odds?" or "Small world!" And of course, I left Taco Bell wondering if I just had a God–Incidence. As I pondered that question, I came up with a 'no' for my answer, I think it was just a coincidence. I realize I could be wrong about that thought. I've heard people say they don't believe anything is a coincidence. I think I understand what they mean, but I'm still undecided on the issue. I would like to clarify what I think does count and some criteria that qualify an incident as a God–Incidence.

I think one or all of these apply to the stories in this book.

1. A need is met.
2. People have a sense of being used by God.
3. Some sort of message is received or communicated.
4. Someone is blessed.

In my encounter with the Taco Bell worker, I didn't feel like any of the four applied, so I wouldn't call it a God–Incidence.

Compare that to my encounters with Coach Jody Ford....

# Coach Ford

I was driving our church bus and hauling kids from a local camp to the swimming pool at Central Methodist University (CMU) for an afternoon cool-off.

After dropping the kids off, I had two hours to myself, so I decided to find an air conditioned room and study for my sermon. I walked up the hill from the pool to the first open building and stepped inside to an empty lounge area where I opened my Bible and journal and began to study and write.

Within about ten minutes a man walked out of an office door and greeted me. I introduced myself to him and told him why I was there. He introduced himself to me as the new head football coach at CMU. I was a middle school football coach and we talked a little football, then he went back to his office and I went back to my studying.

About five minutes later he came back out of the office and said "Hey, would you like to be the team chaplain?" We spoke about the role and agreed to speak later in the week. Thus, I began a four year stint as the team chaplain. Jody and I became friends and I had the opportunity to speak regularly to a great group of young men.

As a result of this 'chance' encounter with Jody, I had the privilege of baptizing Jody and his wife Jill's daughters and I encouraged the faith of many on the team. Jody was diagnosed with cancer while coaching at CMU, and I was able to walk alongside him during his battle.

Unfortunately for me, Jody lost his job at CMU and eventually took another coaching position in Texas. Our friendship continues, but distance makes it harder to stay in touch.

The day we purchased the Jeep Patriot, Kathleen and I were killing time in Columbia waiting for the final inspection and paperwork before making our purchase. We decided to use our time by taking a walk on the trail at Cosmo Park. The lot was pretty empty as I parked my car and we started walking toward the trail. After we had gone a few yards, I heard someone yell, "Gillman!"

I turned around and it was Jody Ford. He 'just happened' to be driving through Cosmo Park reminiscing by himself. He had come back from Texas to visit family and was making some other visits in the Columbia area. He was hoping to contact me and catch up while he was in town. He hopped out and walked a lap with us. We reconnected and caught up on the latest with our families.

I consider this a God–Incidence, different than my encounter with the Taco Bell worker. When I apply the four criteria listed before, here is what I find:

1. Jody and I both have a need for friendship.
2. I feel like God is using me to help Jody's faith and vice versa.
3. I think God communicated a message to me in Cosmo park that he is not done with Jody and I having a relationship.
4. I am blessed by Jody, he is an encourager, family man, and investing in the lives of young men from all over the country. I think he is blessed by me too.

Recognizing God–Incidences has helped reaffirm my faith. I hope these stories will help you see the ways God is working in your life as well.

# Thank You!

To God for moving in noticeable ways in my life and the lives of others in Boone County.

To Harrisburg Christian Church for a sabbatical time to focus on getting this book into print and for funding the project.

To the other story contributors. When I first had the idea of this book, it was my own stories I was most excited to tell. As you began to share your stories with me, that excitement changed and I found myself even more excited to get your stories in print. Thank you for entrusting me with your story.

To my wife, whose faith and prayers have been the backbone of our family's journey together.

To Rod Casey for encouraging me to take a sabbatical and write this book.

To Yolanda Ciolli of AKA–Publishing and Compass Flower Press for helping me publish my first book.

*Soli Deo gloria* (Glory to God alone).


If you have a God–Incidence that you would like to share or if you would be interested in having Pastor John Gillman speak at one of your events, he can be reached by email at pastor@harrisburgchristian.org or call 573.875.5577 to reach him by phone at the Harrisburg Christian Church office.

CPSIA information can be obtained
at www.ICGtesting.com
Printed in the USA
BVHW072054010320
573704BV00005B/18